The
HEART *of*
MINISTRY

DR. TERENCE O. HAYES, SR.

WESTBOW
PRESS®
A DIVISION OF THOMAS NELSON
& ZONDERVAN

This book is a work of non-fiction. Unless otherwise noted, the author and the publisher make no explicit guarantees as to the accuracy of the information contained in this book and in some cases, names of people and places have been altered to protect their privacy.

WestBow Press books may be ordered through booksellers or by contacting:

WestBow Press
A Division of Thomas Nelson & Zondervan
1663 Liberty Drive
Bloomington, IN 47403
www.westbowpress.com
844-714-3454

Because of the dynamic nature of the Internet, any web addresses or links contained in this book may have changed since publication and may no longer be valid. The views expressed in this work are solely those of the author and do not necessarily reflect the views of the publisher, and the publisher hereby disclaims any responsibility for them.

Scripture marked NIV are taken from the Holy Bible, New International Version®. NIV®. Copyright © 1973, 1978, 1984 by International Bible Society. Used by permission of Zondervan. All rights reserved.

Scripture quotations marked NLT are taken from the Holy Bible, New Living Translation, copyright © 1996, 2004, 2015 by Tyndale House Foundation. Used by permission of Tyndale House Publishers, Inc., Carol Stream, Illinois 60188. All rights reserved.

Scripture quotations marked HCSB are taken from the Holman Christian Standard Bible®, Copyright © 1999, 2000, 2002, 2003, 2009 by Holman Bible Publishers. Used by permission. Holman Christian Standard Bible®, Holman CSB®, and HCSB® are federally registered trademarks of Holman Bible Publishers.

Any people depicted in stock imagery provided by Getty Images are models, and such images are being used for illustrative purposes only. Certain stock imagery © Getty Images.

ISBN: 978-1-9736-9846-3 (sc)
ISBN: 978-1-9736-9847-0 (e)

Library of Congress Control Number: 2023909608

Print information available on the last page.

WestBow Press rev. date: 05/24/2023

DEDICATION

This book is dedicated to the love of my life, Rhonda L. Mcduffie-Hayes who has shared the blessings of our lives together forty-three years of holy matrimony. To all of my adult children, Sharita (Carl), Terence (Angel), Shawnda, Alisha (Jarre), Latosha, Troy (Dani), and Tanesha (Brandon); all of you are greatly loved. To all the Hayes' grandchildren, Nana and Papa love you dearly. Lastly, to the Faith Deliverance Church of God in Christ family, I am humbled to serve you.

Dr. David Hirschman—You are a great mentor and brother to me.

Dr. Samuel Paul—My big brother!

To my Stephens family—You loved on my siblings and me after losing our mom-LOVE YOU FOR LIFE!

To my sisters and brother, Rhonda, Karen, Monique, and Craig

To all my pastor friends—We are in this together. Let this book bless you as it has blessed me writing it.

In loving memory of my dearest mother, Ethel Lee Hayes; my heartbeat, my father, Thomas Lee Hayes; my music inspiration. My oldest brother—Stanford-You are greatly missed. My mother-in-law, Helen D. Mcduffie, was a sweet and kind woman who loved me dearly.

The Biblical verse that saved my life:

"Thou wilt keep him in perfect peace, whose mind is stayed on thee: because he trusted in thee. (Isaiah 26:3, KJV)

Take care of your mental health. It's
important. Someone depends on you.

Contents

Introduction

What is Community?

The community is comprised of the people in the surrounding areas who identify the needs, wants, and mindsets necessary for them to thrive and grow in the neighborhood. Professional people, businesses, and health care facilities bring in state of the art training, health awareness, and the willingness and openness to have an educated dialogue on mental illness today. It takes a concerted effort for stakeholders, executive board members, presidents, and diligent workers to be willing to be the leaders and shakers of every changing landscape and keep the right services in our communities. Technology has reshaped the ways in which business is conducted. However, nothing takes the place of the human touch of the doctors and nurses, healthcare workers, professionals, and the workers and families who occupy the brick and mortar places in the local community.

It Is Time!

The time is here to embrace the design and road map of the twenty-first century. We need to be reminded of the history of how health care, education, parenting, families, churches, and neighborhood facilities will make a difference in the everyday lives of ordinary people. It is our hope that this book will enlighten you and take you on a journey that will be rewarding and life changing in the days to come.

The Congregation in a Community

Introduction

Community is defined as a group of people living in the same place or having a particular characteristic in common. The commonality represents the traditional family of mother and father with children, single parents, older men and women, widows and widowers, divorcés and divorcées, and singles. In a community, the daily preparation of working a nine-to-five job brings about a commotion in the four corners of the neighborhood. Children prepare to attend schools—high school, college, or trade school—for academic purposes. Careers are being selected so that people become productive citizens to live their best lives. However, after it's all said and done, there is the one place in a community that brings everyone together to look for the same response and calmness, to rest their souls, and to sit in a position to feed the spiritual person: the church.

In a community, a church is known for many physical features, such as the size of the building, a steeple seen from afar, the landscape of trimmed lawns, the stained glass windows, and a distinguished sign advertising a special community event for all. Yes, this is the place. The bumper sticker says it all: "I love my church!" Loving the church is loving God. Many matters of the heart come against the church, including doctrinal views, denominational views, theological views, and more. The church can be challenged by these points. Of all the many challenges that can come against the church, Jesus Christ made one key declaration about them through his follower Peter: "And I tell you that you are Peter, and on this rock I will build my church, and the gates of Hades will not overcome it" (Matthew 16:18 NIV). This very church is standing in communities across the globe. It has a purpose, it has an identity, and it is not in a crisis, for it is through this church that many lives are affected, touched, and changed.

The content in this book will explore the impact and the influence that the church in a community has in the lives of the men and women who have the discipline and desire to belong to a like-minded family of kindred spirits. Members in a congregation need to have the mind of Christ: "In your relationships with one another, have the same mindset as Christ Jesus" (Philippians 2:5 NIV). Relationships create unity, strength, and the heart of belonging to ensure the work of ministry is done at any cost. The content will further reveal the transformational approach a church has in the lives of congregants who want a life-changing experience with Christ, the change agent for all. A transformational church has a straightforward message—a message of hope. The Book of Lamentations reveals that "The Lord is my portion, saith my soul; therefore will I hope in him" (Lamentations 3:24). Hope is the key that brings serenity and peace to a chaotic situation.

The Importance of Hope

One of the most earth-shattering pandemics hit the world in the winter of 2019 and early 2020. The coronavirus, COVID-19, shook the world. Many churches experienced an awakening and a turning point in navigating the waters of leading churches during these challenging moments in our lifetimes. Leaders had to move forward with hope and faith in God, knowing he was their hope, peace, and protection. Hope was challenged head on, and thousands of lives were lost. How did the world get through this? What made the difference in the final analysis of a crisis such as this? As Paul writes, "If only for this life we have hope in Christ, we are of all people most to be pitied" (1 Corinthians 15:19 NIV). An optimistic view came to a people who had to look beyond the crisis and understand who was really in control. The words of the hymn articulate it like this.

> My hope is built on nothing less,
> than Jesus's blood and righteousness.
> I dare not trust the sweetest frame,
> But wholly lean on Jesus's name.

A transformational church is centered on *hope*. Lastly, a transformational church has one distinguished message: the gospel of Jesus Christ, as revealed from the scriptures, the Holy Word of the Lord. It is the message of the gospel of Jesus Christ that is shouted toward the rafters in the churches in our communities. It is in our sanctuaries that the message from the psalmist is a revival of the soul: "I would have lost heart, unless I had believed that I would see the goodness of the Lord in the land of the living" (Psalm 27:13 NKJV). Pastors stand in pulpits declaring the message of Christ to a dying world looking for a blessed Savior; his name is Jesus. The clear and inerrant word of the gospel sets our hearts ablaze to become the followers and disciples of Jesus Christ. As we read in Romans, "For I am not ashamed of the gospel, because it is the power of God that brings salvation to everyone who believes: first to the Jew, then to the Gentile" (Romans 1:16 NIV).

Transformation

To transform a community, the right message needs to be disseminated on the earth. It can't be diluted. It can't be lessened or stripped of its essence. It needs to be firm, sharper than any two-edged sword, and be the message of the gospel. Let's be realistic: there are false prophets and false teachers who spread bad news in the community. It is almost like the lesson where Jesus was questioned, tested, and challenged by the Pharisees and Sadducees. Nehemiah had to confront men who wanted to take him off his task of building the wall in Jerusalem. He notes "that Sanballat and Geshem sent unto me saying, Come, let us meet together in some of the villages in the plain of Ono. But they thought to do me mischief" (Nehemiah 6:2 KJV). Paul makes this candid point: "But even if we or an angel from heaven should preach a gospel other than the one, we preached to you, let him be under God's curse!" (Galatians 1:8 NIV). Keeping our communities safe is a potent agent that will stand the test of time. Safety is job one.

The Local Church in the Community

The local church in the community is the ingredient that makes the whole concept of attending church meaningful and purposeful. It offers a sense of belonging. However, in belonging, a person needs to feel secure, safe, and wanted. The moment a person approaches a church, everything he or she sees, hears, and senses about the church helps the person decide to settle in or become a member of a particular body. The greatest resource in the church community is the people who comprise the body of Christ—its members at their best. One may ask, "How so?" A church body is not in competition with other churches in a community. There is a church that is the right fit, the right structure, and the right place for you. As Paul writes, "As it is, there are many parts, but one body" (1 Corinthians 12:20 NIV). In a world with over six billion people, can you imagine what the world would be like if everyone was the same—no differences in personalities, skin color, language, or physical appearances? However, God's wisdom and design of humankind did all of us a huge favor. Paul also writes,

> Just as a body, through one, has many parts, but all its many parts forms one body, so it is with Christ. For we were all baptized by one Spirit, so as to form one body-whether Jews or Gentiles, slave or free—and we were all given the one Spirit to drink. Even so the body is not made up of one part but of many. (1 Corinthians 12:12–14 NIV)

This depiction is a gift to a community, a gift wrapped all in the identity of Jesus Christ with diversity and unity. It is the unity of the community that will keep it always moving in the right direction.

The Place You Choose to Worship

A systems approach in addressing the importance of the church in many communities across the globe has what is known as an internal ecosystem. Every church has something that gives it the "it factor," the drawing mechanism, the Spirit-filled setting. The early church in the book of Acts was the birth of something big happening in the lives of a group of men and women. Jesus Christ instructed them before his ascension to tarry or wait in Jerusalem and be endowed with power from on high. You see, God's presence is vital and necessary for having an emotional and soul-stirring experience. In his letter, Paul writes, "Do you not know that your bodies are temples of the Holy Spirit, who is in you, whom you have received from God? You are not your own" (1 Corinthians 6:19). The early church upper room encounter ushered in a presence that connected all who were joined in the room, with a purposeful language interruption that hit the community. They were speaking in one another's language by the divine outpouring of the Holy Spirit. This is what makes a congregation unified. Something like an upper room experience made all the difference in the operation and functionality of the church. The presence and spirit of God is the lifeline for the church to thrive and survive. I don't know about you, but if God is not in the building where I am worshipping, I'll take the high road like Moses.

> Then Moses said to him, "If your Presence does not go with us, do not send us up from here. How will anyone know that you are pleased with me and with your people unless you go with us? What else will distinguish me and your people from all the other people on the face of the earth?" (Exodus 33:15–16)

Building a Mass Community to Nurture Congregational Vitality

Introduction

One of the notable observations in a community is to see how well it grows and spreads its wings as people come from all over the area to comprise what is known as "our community." It becomes an established place where the people take ownership and occupancy, and have a take-charge attitude and a sense of belonging. In taking ownership of a community, one must foster a great depth of pride. You can lift your head, stick your chest out and shout it on the rooftop, "What a feeling to belong to this community." Under this mantra, a congregation becomes better, wiser, and more vital because it matters most when it's taken personally.

Nurture is defined as "the process of caring for and encouraging the growth and development of someone or something."[1] It takes a caring attitude, a warm spirit of interest, and compassion to see a community grow and enlarge itself to have a significant impact and influence on the lives of all persons concerned. It

---

[1] *Encyclopedia.com*, s.v. "nurture," accessed April 27, 2023, https://www.encyclopedia.com/social-sciences-and-law/sociology-and-social-reform/sociology-general-terms-and-concepts/nurture.

takes nurturing not only to develop a community; nurturing has a solid spiritual foundation.

In Ephesians, we read, "Fathers, do not exasperate your children; instead, bring them up in the training and instruction of the Lord" (Ephesians 6:4 NIV). All the necessary approaches, processes, and ideas to establish a vital community in a congregation must be purposeful. The pastor of a congregation must adeptly and sensitively provide the care, nurturing, and attention needed to ensure the members in the congregation are growing in the knowledge and grace of our Lord Jesus Christ.

Within a growing and vital ministry in the surrounding community, I serve as Senior Pastor of Faith Deliverance Church of God in Christ. "The church is a Pentecostal ministry, and the founder is an aged gentleman who loves God and family life." The founder's words are "to have good churches; you need good homes." The people who come to a church from their own personal home space are what makes the success or growth of a church. Let's continue with this good church theme. Psalm 127 states, "Unless the Lord builds the house, the builders labor in vain. Unless the Lord watches over the city, the guards stand watch in vain" (Psalm 127:1 NIV). Families make the churches we attend the places we love to bring our families and friends. In thriving churches, a pastor may implement a Friends and Family Day, a Back to Church Campaign, and other structured ideas to create a stirring in the people's hearts to enter the doors of the church. This is one of the many ways church growth comes to life in a community. Creativity is essential to see things like this take place.

Language in Community

One of the most significant impacts the early church had was in bringing people from different backgrounds together in a common interest. The early church experienced exponential growth. It was a vital force after the gospel of Jesus was preached by Peter. As recounted in Acts, "Peter replied, 'Repent and be baptized, every one of you, in the name of Jesus Christ for the forgiveness of your sins. And you will receive the gift of the Holy Spirit'" (Acts 2:38–39 NLT). It was here the church's congregation in the community grew. Over three thousand souls were added to it. That had to be an encouraging moment. The Bible describes how the church came together and unified to be a beacon of light in the community. A community needs beacons of light to shine that will draw others to Christ. Additionally, in Acts we read, "And they continued steadfastly in the apostles' doctrine and fellowship, in the breaking of bread, and prayers" (Acts 2:42). In a community with the church, there needs to be sound teaching and words that cannot be condemned to bring solid principles of faith.

One of the most fulfilling aspects of the church is having the means to fellowship. Fellowship is coming together. There has to be an outlet for families to connect, for people to come together who may be experiencing life situations so they don't need to feel isolated or alone. The early church made being together a priority. One of the joys of receiving Christ is feeling welcomed and having a sense of belonging. Lastly, prayer is vital in the community. If there was ever a time in today's communities for worship to be rendered, it is now. Prayer is talking to God about the things that are affecting the daily problems of living. Congregations in communities pray for unity and peace in the neighborhood. They draw their forces together in times of crisis, natural disaster, caring for the homeless, and more.

The Character of a Leader in Community

The character and charisma of leaders in a community makes people aware that someone close to the people's hearts is reachable and touchable. Pastors need to be relatable. We read in Jeremiah,

"And I will give you shepherds after my own heart, who will guide you with knowledge and understanding" (Jeremiah 3:15 NLT). In crisis, stress, and other family-related issues, the church has a body of believers who live amongst them in the community. Many attend churches in their communities. Paul had excellent care and love for the Church of Thessalonica. Paul was bold in his faith and beliefs and wanted to ensure the members were given the guidance and direction they needed. He writes, "For we speak as messengers approved by God to be entrusted with the Good News. Our purpose is to please God, not people. He alone examines the motives of our hearts" (1 Thessalonians 2:4 NLT). The church needs true disciples who will get into the trenches and show love and support for developing followers in the Kingdom of God. They do this through good instruction and teaching from the scriptures the way of the Lord.

Paul was indeed an example of this behavior. He gave the illustration of how a mother provides the nurturing and care of her children. He writes, "As apostles of Christ, we certainly had a right to make some demands of you, but instead we were like children among you. Or we were like a mother feeding and caring for her children" (1 Thessalonians 2:7 NLT). People will never understand the heart of a leader in the community until they see that that person cares. An opportunity awaits pastors and leaders in the community to rise and show what real love and authentic compassion look like. One may ask," How do I find answers to live a life free from sin? How do I establish a deep and meaningful relationship with Christ?" It's in these moments a leader makes time for administering the word of God in a community by having in place a good night of Bible study.

One of the mainstays in ministry is Sunday School. Sunday School brings the congregation in a unified setting with various teachers instructing the students through the word of God. Sunday School today is on the cutting edge with today's technology and different teaching resources. Many churches set aside a day during

THE HEART OF MINISTRY

the week that is strictly reserved for the word of God to be explained. It's a time of giving, sharing, and being attentive to the men and women who make time to make their way to the house of God. Paul made it clear: "We loved you so much that we shared with you not only God's Good News but our own lives too" (1 Thessalonian 2:8 NLT). Can you see the heart of a leader like Paul in your community? Have you witnessed the unselfishness and untiring level of sacrifice and dedication in a leader in your community? The word on the street, the word in the community is "there is something great happening in our neighborhood." The church's mission is meeting the needs of everyday people and the betterment of their souls. There should be a genuine presence of soul care in all churches in our neighborhoods.

Paul writes, "Never once did we try to win you with flattery, as you well know. And God is our witness that we were not pretending to be your friends just to get your money" (1 Thessalonians 2:5 NLT). The leadership in the life of Paul was exemplary and greatly admired.

Some situations will prevent a good opportunity from happening in a community. Every community has needs. Some needs are more pressing or urgent than others. Years ago, there was a saying that "If you can't beat city hall, join them." Today's pastors are joining school boards, becoming community activists, running for mayor, and so on. There is nothing new under the sun. Paul encountered opposition from the church of Thessalonica. He was separated from them not by choice but by the intense climate of opposition and unrest. He writes,

> Dear brothers and sisters, after we were separated
> from you for a little while (though our hearts
> never left you), we tried very hard to come back
> because of our intense longing to see you again...
> We wanted very much to come to you, and I,

Paul, tried again and again, but Satan prevented us. (1 Thessalonians 2:17–18)

In events such as this, leaders can make the community better when forces make ways to prevent growth, opportunity, and change taking place. There are zoning laws when a new building or structure is in the works. Someone will, and make no mistake about it, be opposed to see God's kingdom rise and expand. However, in this case, Paul was aware of what was taking place. He sent good men he knew could be just as vital and relevant as if he was there. You need intelligent and vigilant people on a team to get a job done. Paul sent Timothy. This is the beginning of a mentoring moment in the community. Who can you send when you are not available to get a job done? How well have you developed others to lead in your absence? Paul told them, "'We sent Timothy to visit you.' He is our brother and God's co-worker in proclaiming the Good News of Christ" (1 Thessalonians 3:2 NLT).

Mentoring Others in a Community

Former senator and presidential nominee Hillary Rodman Clinton once said, "It takes a village to raise a child." This African American proverb embraces the concept that an entire community takes on the responsibility to make a difference in a child's life. In a village, many great men and women have roles in sharing, caring, training, empowering, and making a difference in the lives of all those who come across their paths. This is the leadership Paul exhibited in the village he led. He drew disciples to Christ and mentored men in ministry to step into situations. One of the admirable characteristics of the forty-fourth President of the United States, Barack H. Obama, was that he was a community organizer. He knew how to get into the trenches of involvement in a community. He knew how to organize a body of people to help him win his campaign as a senator and achieve the highest office in the land as president of the free world. God needs people in a community who can rise, take up a challenge, and bring great things to life. Our communities don't have to fail. They can become agents of change, communities of great resolve and resilience, successful in every challenge and endeavor they may face.

Paul mentored young Timothy. After once denying the way of Christ, Paul had his own personal experience on the road of Damascus. Paul went abroad threatening anyone who called on the name of Christ. However, when there is a God-given role or destiny on your life, nothing you do can change it. In the community, persons will be sought after to do work that will make the work even stronger and more purposeful. No person is an island. A community cannot reach its fullest potential unless the individuals rise and take charge of the needs of the people for that moment.

Paul went on to Derbe and Lystra, where there was a disciple named Timothy. He was the son of a believing Jewish woman, but his father was a Greek (Acts 16:1 CSB). Timothy was helped to do great work in the churches in the community, and "So the churches were strengthened in the faith and grew daily in numbers" (Acts 16:5 CSB). Mentoring produced growth in this community. The work needed someone available to nurture, instruct, and provide guidance along the way. Churches can thrive and survive when all players are in place and all the pieces are aligned rightfully to fit the design and demographics of the community. This approach only happens with foresight, emotional intelligence, and the maturity needed to bring people together. A strengthened church means a strengthened faith. The ultimate design for churches to display is one of great faith and great strength. This is a winning combination every time.

The church grew numerically from the truth delivered amongst the people. In many churches today, the established programs provide services that people in the community may need, such as support groups, help with alcohol and drug addictions, and other matters of life. The church should never be a place of outcast. It is for the lost, the brokenhearted, and the hurting. God's church is designed to grow. The early church grew daily as the gospel of Jesus Christ was being preached. The same principle applies for today's church for it to grow and advance the work of the Lord.

The Impact of Women in a Community

Ministry includes both men and women. The women who prepared the Lord's body after his death on the cross. John writes, "Early on the first day of the week, while it was still dark, Mary Magdalen went to the tomb and saw that the stone had been removed from the entrance" (John 20:1 NIV). Jesus's ministry had a huge impact on women. They loved him, served him, were obedient to his words, and many had servants' hearts. In today's communities, the work and skills of women bring great structure, order, and guidance. Paul was on a mission to make the churches around the globe beacons of light and hope. On his journey to Philippi, seeking a place to pray, he encountered a woman by the name of Lydia, whose role made a difference in the community where she lived.

In Acts, we read, "On the Sabbath we went outside the city gate to the river, where we expected to find a place of prayer. We sat down and began to speak to the women who had gathered there" (Acts 16:13). It is worth noting the prayer in this account. Prayer is simply communicating, talking to God. Every community needs people in it to offer prayers for the needs of the community. In the lives of women, prayer is rendered fervently and effectually. Prayer changes things. It's that simple. The words of Jesus Christ to his disciples were clear, precise, and specific:

"Therefore, I tell you, whatever you ask for in prayer, believe that you receive it, and it will be yours" (Mark 11:24 NIV).

Paul met a woman by the name of Lydia. She is described as a dealer in purple cloth from the city of Thyatira and a worshipper of God. A powerful thing happened to Lydia in her community when Paul came into her life: "The Lord opened her heart to respond to Paul's message. When she and the members of her household were baptized, she invited us to her home" (Acts 16:14–15 NIV). Who have you invited into your home in your community? What kind gesture of warm hospitality have you extended to your neighbor? Many churches in communities offer outreach events that bring people into their places of worship. These include Men's Breakfast, Community Day, Back to Church Sunday, and Friends and Family Day. These are just a few opportunities to show the hospitable spirit in churches around the world. The behind-the-scenes person who desires to see these days come forth is the pastor. He or she wants to "share with the Lord's people who are in need. Practice hospitality" (Romans 12:13 NIV). There is always a need in someone's life. These needs are met in the community.

In these moments, the outcome of good mentorship rises in a community. There is a great spiritual moment here that cannot be overlooked. If Paul had never traveled to Thyatira, this may not have occurred. Someone is waiting on you to affect that person's life right now; you just do not know it. As Lydia tells Paul, "'If you consider me a believer in the Lord,' she said, 'come and stay at my house.' And she persuaded us" (Acts 16:15 NIV). Our communities will become what they are destined to be when the mentor shows up at the right time in a person's life. The mentor's assignment is to serve as the trusted voice of experience, offer wise counsel, and be the sounding board to hear and guide when direction is needed. Trust needs to be the sustaining characteristic in mentors across the board. The truth of the matter is that you simply can't trust everyone. When there are no good mentors in

DR. TERENCE O. HAYES, SR.

the community, this is what happens: "For lack of guidance a nation falls, but victory is won through many advisers" (Proverbs 11:14 NIV). Note the mention of "many advisers." The more support provided in the community, the better the results.

The Community Out of Control

The socialization of a community takes on a whole new meaning with the outcome and end roads of the activities that take place. In today's culture, there is more discussion about human rights, civil rights, sexuality, freedom of speech, and more. As soon as you encounter one life event, another arises seemingly overnight. The landscape shifted abruptly with the death of George Floyd. The taking of a man's life recorded on a cellphone left many in tears, hurt, and confused. The face of racism was being played out in living color right inside homes and communities in America. As we read in Acts, "From one man he made every nation of men, that they should inhabit the whole earth; and he determined the times set for them and the exact places whey they should live" (Acts 17:26). God created us all from the same cloth. Sin has created more problems and issues than necessary. How a person sees color is painful at best. From the archives of the Bible, prejudices and racism are nothing new. In Ecclesiastes, we read, "Again, I looked and saw all the oppression that was taking place under the sun: I saw the tears of the oppressed, and they have no comforter; power was on the side of their oppressors, and they have no comforter" (Ecclesiastes 4:1 NIV).

The agony and optics of hate and social injustice have put a painful stain on our world. The streets became the place for people expressing themselves to protest the wrong. A protest is defined as "a statement or action expressing disapproval of or objection to something." Riots, demonstrations, and people wanting to be

THE HEART OF MINISTRY

seen and heard are revealed in the history of the word of God. Dr. Martin Luther King, Jr, stated, "Nonviolence is a powerful and just weapon, which cuts without wounding and ennobles the man who wields it. It is a sword that heals." The approach of nonviolence is the way of safe, God-fearing communities.

A community with many social relationship issues was the church at Corinth. The community had many problems that could have quickly destroyed it. It was out of control, its people engaged in drinking, sexual promiscuity, and more. Paul brought the message of Jesus Christ to this community in need of a life-changing experience. Paul's approach toward this congregation was that of a caring pastor who wanted to help bring the people to a place of civility, holiness, and righteousness. Note his words: "I always thank God for you because of his grace given you in Christ Jesus. For in him you have been enriched in every way—in all your speaking, and in all your knowledge—because our testimony about Christ was confirmed in you" (1 Corinthians 1:4–6 NIV). People who are striving to live Christian lives need to have hearts of love and compassion. As a person is introduced to the way of Christ, there needs to be a leader, a voice that is patient, kind, and understanding, to bring the person to the place where learning the ways of Christ will impact him or her.

One of the issues in this church was division. Division in a community causes strife and disharmony. You can accomplish more being unified than you can being divided. Paul's message to the Corinthian church was clear: "I appeal to you, brothers, in the name of our Lord Jesus Christ, that all of you agree with one another so that there may be no divisions among you and that you may be perfectly united in mind and thought" (1 Corinthians 1:10 NIV). Unity brings all minds to work toward a common goal. Involving everyone together in seeing the big picture will produce a better outcome for all concerned.

A community in the city of Dayton, Ohio came together to develop a marketplace. The project came to fruition through a few people who had a mind to work together. The plans were drawn, the complex came together, and in time, it celebrated its grand opening right in the heart of the community. Unlike your typical grocery store, the workers, customers, and supporters of the community own this complex. This is a strong demonstration of a body of people working together in a shared community to bring a vision to pass. Note the phrasing of a "shared community." Taking ownership, putting a stake into the ground, making an investment, and pouring into a community brings a shared community essence into play. Community members who once had to travel across town to a grocery store can now travel a few blocks or minutes away in their own area. Vision is powerful; it is life-changing, and it can make the impossible become a real possibility.

As other matters of the heart took place with this church community, there were signs of favoritism. Jealousy, envy, and quarreling rose among the people. Paul asked questions to make the community look within itself for answers to a problem. He asked, "For since there is jealousy and quarreling among you, are you not worldly? Are you not acting like mere men?" (1 Corinthians 3:3 NIV). Just as communication is vital in all day-to-day relationships, it is as important to be candid and confront issues in the community. There are moments when you speak truth to power. These moments are excellent examples of making communities more substantial and better through mature and responsible conversations. Making a difference is a strong theme of this chapter. Different circumstances will bring about different responses. In an ideal world, everything would be perfect; there would be no issues, no drama, and no dysfunctional attitudes. However, this is a fallen world. Sin is the cause of it all. It all began in the first community God created at the beginning of time: the Garden of Eden.

The Garden of Eden is the first community where problems occurred that brought disorder and chaos to the land. In this community, God hoped for peace and harmony to exist. We read that "The Lord God took the man and put him in the Garden of Eden to work it and take care of it" (Genesis 2:15 NIV). Taking care of a community is vital for its growth and success. From the least to the greatest of attention to detail for all the elements that comprise a healthy community is relevant for the thriving and sustainment of the environment. This community was comprised of Adam and the animals. Adam needed to have someone compatible with him who could be relatable and identifiable. As the Book of Genesis states,

> But for Adam, no suitable helper was found. So, the Lord God caused the man to fall into a deep sleep, and while he was sleeping, he took one of man's ribs and closed the place with flesh. Then the Lord God made a woman from the rib he had taken out of the man, and he brought her to the man. (Genesis 2:20–22)

This is where God stepped in and provided a helpmeet: a woman. What takes place after the design of the woman was the beginning of a community fitly designed for man and woman.

This community in Eden was one of complete order. There were no wild plants or grains growing on the earth in its beginning. There was no rain to fall from the sky until after the fall. God used springs to water the things on the earth. The pleasantries of life manifested in Eden. To keep this garden in good standing, God gave Adam a specific instruction: "And the Lord God commanded the man, 'You are free to eat from any tree in the garden, but you must not eat from the tree of the knowledge of good and evil, for when you eat from it you will certainly die'" (Genesis 2:16–17 NIV). A community can't just spring up out of nowhere without rules, laws, or regulations. People's lives can be endangered from lack of boundaries and measures in place to keep the community civil and safe. It all came crashing down after the fall.

The fall brought sin into the world. The fall brought hardship, pain, labor, and chaos into God's perfect world. This is where the lack of accountability raised its head in the community. There was blaming, not taking responsibility for one's actions, and finger pointing. How many times have you witnessed community leaders caught up in scandal for embezzlement, bribery, adultery, and other matters that cause hurt and disbelief in the community? God's plan was for a perfect world, but the fall changed these hopes of a world free from sin.

However, all is not lost. There is a place of restoration and forgiveness. It is when the real men and women stand up and face the repercussions of their actions to allow healing to take place for the betterment of a community.

Counsel in a Community

The community is more than just a place to gather, engage, and interact. It is a place of imparting wisdom, knowledge, good skillsets, and more. There is a certain season or time of year when the men and women who live in a community will seek or run for a public office. What better place than in the community for an official to become the next politician, governor, administrator of schools, and yes, even president of the United States. Everything has a beginning. Everyone has that someone, that person who influenced that person to take that challenge or risk or to pursue a dream. This brings me to share the importance of wise counsel in a community. We read in Proverbs, "Without counsel purposes are disappointed: but in the multitude of counselors, they are established" (Proverbs 15:22 KJV). There is a lot of wisdom right before you in people who you see daily. There should never be a time when you are without direction.

THE HEART OF MINISTRY

There is a leader in the Bible whose character set him high above his peers. His name is Moses. We learn that "Moses was a very humble man, more humble than anyone else on the face of the earth" (Numbers 12:3 NIV). That's a tall order to be acknowledged as the meekest and most humble man on the face of the earth. This man had favor with God. It takes acceptance to accomplish things, and it takes acceptance to open doors that only God will provide. However, with this noted personality trait, Moses needed some direction to help him succeed. He was heading in the wrong direction. You will find yourself going in the wrong direction by the failure to yield to sound advice. Moses had the tremendous task of leading the Israelites through the many challenges and obstacles they encountered in the wilderness. Pharaoh had challenged him because he didn't want to let the people of God go. Finally, after all that took place, Pharaoh and his army of men were drowned at sea as they gathered to destroy the people of God. It was the leadership and fortitude of Moses that granted God's people victory.

At another point in their lives, the people became a burden to Moses. As much as Moses loved God, the people who were following Moses did not always seemingly love God as much as he did. In all of this, Moses simply said to the Lord, "Why have you brought this trouble on your servant? What have I done to displease you that you put the burden of all these people on me?" (Numbers 11:11 NIV). It appears this had become a burdensome task. It almost seems Moses was having a meltdown from all he had encountered with serving and leading. He concluded the conversation with God by saying, "Did I conceive all these people? Did I give them birth? Why do you tell me to carry them in my arms, as a nurse carries an infant, to the land you promised on oath to their forefathers?" (Numbers 11: 12 NIV). Let's turn the focus of all this to wise counsel in the community.

Moses's father-in-law noticed that the behavior of this meek, humble leader needed intervention. Simply put, he saw that Moses was overwhelmed leading God's people. If you are a pastor in ministry, an elder, or missionary, let this moment speak to your heart. How he intervened highlights the need for and importance of community. Jethro gave Moses good administrative advice to organize the people he was leading more effectively and efficiently. The guidance also included how to handle disputes. The formula was laid and set, and all Moses needed to do was accept it. Instances like this will make or break a leader in a community going down the wrong path. Moses's intentions were good; the people were going against him as a person. You can't be a lone ranger and expect to come out on top of your game. Let's explore further the details of what took place with the conversation of Moses and Jethro, one of the most potent interventions of communication in leadership.

Moses's behavior caught the eye of Jethro. It is essential to note you are always on display. Someone is always watching you even when you don't know it. Jethro took the lead and began the conversation with Moses, asking, "What is this you are doing for the people? Why do you alone sit as a judge, while all these people stand around you from morning till evening?" (Exodus 18:14 NIV). Moses answered him, "Because the people come to me to seek God's will. Whenever they have a dispute, it is brought to me, and I decide between the parties and inform them of God's decree and instructions" (Exodus 18:16 NIV). This all seems like it's harmless. It seems Moses is doing what many leaders today do: give advice and counsel to the people who follow them. Here's the question. What do you do when someone tells you, "What you are doing is not good" (Exodus 18:17 NIV)? Take note—all people can't speak into your life because their motives may not be pure. You should have an inner circle of trusted and respected men and women you welcome to speak into your life. This is where good counsel takes place in the community. Jethro further tells Moses, "You and these people who come to you will only wear yourselves out. The work is too heavy for you; you cannot handle it alone. Listen to me, and I will give you some advice, and may God be with you" (Exodus 18:18–19 NIV). The advice given to Moses from his father-in-law was not to distract from the leadership Moses had. It was only helping him to be a more effective and stronger leader exercising more disciplined and sound leadership. There are two types of criticism: constructive and destructive. Value anyone who has your best interest at heart in the community.

In addressing the topic of counseling in a community, here is a word for pastors. Forty percent of individuals who are experiencing a mental health crisis will seek the counsel of pastors before a professional counselor. You should have an awareness of how to counsel someone who is in a crisis. You should be a safe person to whom the person may voice his or her concern. Don't be too alarmed. Suppose it is a matter that is beyond your scope of expertise. You are to do your due diligence by making a referral to a licensed professional counselor. You are trained to serve as a pastor, and the counselor is trained to be a counselor. Both of you are great resources in a community.

As an advocate for anyone who encounters the loss of a loved one by suicide, I had to find a way to get to a safe place in my own life. I suffered with suicide ideation, feared ending my own life, and lived in fear that what happened to my mother would happen to me. It has been fifty years since this tragedy impacted my life. Today I am healed in my soul. The memory of my mother will always be part of me.

My Own Story (Eleven-Year-Old Survivor of Suicide)

In 1973, I experienced one of the most tragic events a child could ever encounter. My mom died by suicide. I walked the halls from middle school to high school, hiding the loss of my mother. In my mind, I felt shame and guilt and carried the weight of my mom's death at a very young age. It wasn't until I became an adult and began journaling about my childhood experience that I found my voice to address the topic of suicide. One of my high school peers noted on a Facebook post, "I didn't know you went through this while in school."

I had a successful career in the United States Air Force and retired as a master sergeant from Wright Patterson Air Force Base in my hometown of Dayton, Ohio. After I retired, I wanted to enter a college classroom to obtain a college degree. At the age of forty-nine, I started pursuing a higher level of learning. I selected psychology for a personal reason: to gain an insight into what took place in my mother's life. I began at Park University to obtain an associate's degree. I had been out of school for so long that I took one step at a time to know what college would be like. In the winter of 2011, my journey began. While reading *Charisma* magazine, I saw an advertisement from Liberty University, a Christian university. This was the place where I achieved my academic dreams. I transferred from Park University and finished my tenure with Liberty University. In 2013, I obtained my associate's degree. In 2014, I obtained my bachelor's degree. The love of learning continued; in 2016, I completed my master's degree. All of these were in the field of psychology and Christian counseling. It was the final decision that I wanted to pursue a terminal degree. In the Spring of 2017, I was accepted into the doctoral program at Liberty University, which is where all these degrees were obtained.

As I got closer to finishing, I wanted to do something in memory of my mother. The study of mental health issues, disorders, behaviors, suicide, and more were topics I learned in the classroom. In some strange way, it gave me more confidence and a clearer understanding of what my mom may have gone through in the twenty-nine years of her life. During it all, my faith in God carried me through the tragedy. I often share a passage in the scriptures that was my saving grace: "Thou will keep him in perfect peace whose mind is stayed on thee" (Isaiah 26:3). I completed my doctoral degree in the fall of 2020 and graduated with a 3.86 GPA. At that moment, I established the Ethel Hayes Destigmatization of Mental Health Scholarship. This scholarship became a voice for me to speak candidly about mental health issues. I wanted to confront a stigma in the African American community. You don't have to carry the weight of your pain in silence; seek counseling, seek professional help. As a pastoral counselor, I understand that 40 percent of individuals seek the help of a pastor before seeking assistance from a licensed professional counselor.

The website www.bold.org became the vehicle to get the word out to high school and college students to make an application for the scholarship. The scholarship has awarded over $18,000 to seven high school and college students since its inception in the fall of 2020. This is an ongoing endeavor that I will continue throughout my life. The donors and supporters of this work are dear to my heart. Students write essays to share their worldviews of mental health and how it has impacted their lives or the lives of their loved ones. "I didn't want to see another 11-year-old boy or girl experience the trauma I did as a male." This scholarship allowed me to give back to the community and carry on my mom's memory. Your mental health is essential. Don't hide behind a mask; help is available.

The Importance of Gaining Internal and External Demographic Data on the Congregation and Community

Introduction

The layout and map of a community are intricate parts that make a community vibrant and enticing. Let's define community: "a group of people living in the same place or having a particular characteristic in common. It is also known as a feeling of fellowship with others due to sharing common attitudes, interests, and goals." A kindred spirit, connection, and common goals and views make all the difference in making things happen and bringing groups of people together. It is not easy to get a whole body of people together to reach one common objective, but it can be done with the right approach and focus.

Bringing People Together

As a former military member, one of the most excellent means of bringing a group of people together is in a training environment known as basic training. In this environment, the training instructors have one purpose: to get all the troops to march together in unison, with precision, rhythm, and in-step.

Let's use the Air Force as a point of reference. I served twenty-one years and seven months in this branch and loved every moment of the years of service. You have people catching airplanes to get to the mighty state of Texas. The dress code looks like fashion from the world's four corners, the west coast, east coast, north, and south. Some will be dressed warmly depending on the year and the season, like fall or winter. All of them have lived in their environments. However, to adapt to a new and changing environment, the people must conform to where they will be living for six to eight weeks. The troops are known as rainbows: different patterns and colors. After everyone arrives is when the transformation begins. All the males are lined up for haircuts. For humor, the barber asks, "How do you want it?" Then the razor cuts with no shape or style in mind; all the measures taken are to make everyone look the same. As time progresses, everything you do is as a unit, making you function in the community as a soldier.

Making a Community Strong

Fast forward to the final product. You have practiced drills day in and day out. You have marched to every building or place to conduct your business affairs as a military soldier: recreation, training, dining, medical care, and more. You have been gearing up for the big day: the marching parade for graduation. You have worn the battle dress uniform most of the stay but wearing the dress blues or Class A uniform is the moment you have worked so hard for. Nothing is more exciting and perfect to observe than hundreds of troops marching together in a parade at the sound of a drumbeat, heels clicking, and the voices of training instructors echoing, "Hut two three four, pride, honor, flight." How did this all happen to intentionally make you a soldier? As Paul writes, "No one serving as a soldier gets entangled in civilian affairs but rather tries to please his commanding officer. Similarly, anyone who competes as an athlete does not receive the victor's crown except by competing according to the rules" (2 Timothy 2:4–5 NIV). This is what makes a community strong: pulling together, working together, and serving together. A community has a government. It has municipalities, safety, and town halls. It has entertainment, recreation, medical, healthcare, and mental health facilities, and more. In all of this, there needs to be people, places, and things to bring it all together.

Gathering Data

In gathering data for communities, one must know the community's elements. There are three types: urban, rural, and suburban. Each of the three districts offers what one may need to search for help, guidance, and assistance in a given situation. The navigational system, or the GPS, is paramount to navigating through the terrain of a community. One of the first things a person does in preparing for a road trip is to pull up the destination location. It is the same mindset for finding what you need to meet a community's needs.

Urban Communities

An urban community is developed. There are structures in place, houses are everywhere, there are apartment complexes, and more. You will find businesses and establishments in urban communities to serve the community's needs. An urban community is a fast track to get around the city with highways, roads, and bridges. Many suitable jobs can be found in the heart of an urban community. The population of society in this atmosphere is high.

Suburban Communities

A suburban community comprises towns, small cities, villages, and the like. In these areas, you will find places of government, local fire departments, and most schools. Many who live in the suburbs commute or travel to work to their jobs in the city. A lot of your restaurants and retail establishments are in suburban communities. A suburban community is always in a thriving mode. New businesses are opening, as are food establishments, apartment complexes, housing developments, and more. The financial gains in a suburban community are what city and government officials want to see a rise in. Dollars poured into a community sustain the lifeline of the environment for years to come.

Rural Communities

Rural communities have smaller populations of people than in other communities. The landscape is spread out; homes are distant from each other. There are more agricultural sites, farms, or ranches. These communities can be getaways from the hustle and bustle of everyday life. There is less noise, less traffic, and places for solitude and comfort. People who move into these communities are here by choice. Many have lived in other communities convenient for jobs and for raising families. However, as life progresses and time moves forward, a rural community offers a more settled and calming atmosphere. A rural community has a solitary environment. Jesus Christ traveled the streets of the communities and witnessed men and women from all walks of life. However, when he wanted to find a place less traveled, he found what he wanted in solitary places. As we read in the Gospel of Mark, "Very early in the morning, while it was still dark, Jesus got up, left the house, and went off to a solitary place, where he prayed" (Mark 1:35 NIV).

The GPS (Global Positioning System) in Community

Have you been planning a trip and are excited to get to a place you have never been before? One of the famous sites across the country is AAA. Yes! AAA provides navigation, maps, roadmaps, and atlases to help get you from point A to B. These services are still present. However, in this twenty-first century, there is the GPS (Global Positioning System), which is digital and one of the most used systems for travel. The GPS is a United States-owned utility that provides users with positioning, navigation, and timing (PNT) services. This system has three essential segments: the space segment, the control segment, and the user segment. The space segment has a twenty-four satellite operating system that transmits one-way signals. These provide the correct GPS functioning position and the right time. The control system is like a mass worldwide monitoring control station that ensures all satellites and the maneuvering commands and clocks are all locked and loaded. It further tracks the satellites, keeps information uploaded, and maintains the mechanics and other essential functions of the control system. Lastly, the user segment comprises the GPS receiver equipment that gets the signals from the GPS systems and takes this information to calculate the functioning of the tasks. Just as this GPS is used to control the world, our communities need to have their GPS in our towns, cities, neighborhoods, rural, suburban, and local communities.

A community can be no stronger than its weakest link. In moments of weakness and strength, minds come together to ensure all pieces of the puzzle are identified, located, and placed correctly. One of the most significant descriptions of how each community is recognized by the churches located in the community can be found in the book of Revelation. The seven churches all knew of God, but they didn't function as though they knew him. It can be puzzling and disturbing when unity, togetherness, and guidance are open to all, but only a few adhere or comply. One of the sure ways to help alleviate and resolve these types of problematic issues is by instituting an excellent GPS for a community. A community will exceed, succeed, and proceed to bring forth all the energy and dynamics to be vital for all connected and for the church located there.

The Demographics of
the Seven Churches

Introduction

This section of the book is to share the involvement, engagement, and hands-on approach of a congregation in the community. The community has been defined; the road map has been transferred and followed. It is a known fact: no two neighborhoods are alike. Each of them has its distinct markings that distinguish their differences. In Asia, there were seven churches whose identities depicted how they survived in the community. These communities were explicitly described by letters. John was the writer of Revelation. It's noted John addressed each letter to the "angel of the church." The angel represents the leader, the head of the place. The letters further discussed the state of each church and how each church functioned in the cities. After the observation, John judged each church and gave spiritual advice for its success and for leaning on the word of God for its future. In all the churches, one person is the center: Christ. In our communities, Christ must be front and center of the work we do. Christ is the glue that keeps the churches together. He is the agent for change, transformation, progression, and assimilation to ensure everyone's role has been touched by the hand of God.

A community cannot operate to its fullest potential with envy, strife, or a schism in the body.

Ephesus

Ephesus is the first church mentioned in Revelation. The church was in a prominent and vital city of the Roman province in Asia. It had one of the largest, most affluent banking centers in its part in the world. The writer writes,

> I know all the things you do. I have seen your hard work and your patient endurance. I know you don't tolerate evil people. You have examined the claims of those who say they are apostles but are not. You have discovered they are liars. You have patiently suffered for me without quitting. (Revelation 2:2–3)

This is commendable; their work is not unnoticed, however, everything is not where it should be. As John notes, "I have this complaint against you." Whenever things in a community are not going well, someone must be the fix-it person. This church community didn't have the love it needed to survive. John writes, "You don't love me or each other as you did at first!" You only have one chance to make lasting impressions. However, when you choose to teach the gospel, it must be genuine and acceptable.

Smyrna

Smyrna is the second church. It was small, but it was faithful and dedicated to God even with the difficulties it encountered. It was a seaport community. "I know about your suffering and your poverty—but you are rich! I know the blasphemy of those opposing you. The socio-economic status of this church was in better shape than it realized. It had some poverty, but it was holding its own in wealth. This church was about to face a trial. In many communities, issues can cause concern or havoc in the community, but one must stay focused, committed, and finish the task at hand. John writes, "The devil will throw some of you into prison to test you, you will suffer for ten days. But if you remain faithful even when facing death, I will give you a crown of life" (Revelation 2:10 NLT).

There are times when all you do in a community can seem fruitless or of no value. The hard work, dedication, and resources you pour into it can appear to be overlooked, but in the reading, a crown will be awarded. There is an award awaiting you for all you do. Keep serving and building up the community you are in. Fight for the right resources needed to make your community stronger.

Pergamum

The third church is known as the compromising church, Pergamum. This city was an early capital of a Roman province. One of its noted landscapes was its famous library, along with the animal skins the people used for writing. John writes, "I know that you live in the city where Satan has his throne, yet you have remained loyal to me; you refused to deny me even when Antipas, my faithful witness, was martyred among you there in Satan's City" (Revelation 2:13 NLT). However, God had something against this church: its tolerance of unsound doctrine, teaching, and principles. If there is one thing that can destroy a community, it is unfounded and far-fetched thinking and negative influences. Not everyone is your friend, and neither do they all hope for you to win.

Paul addressed this same problem to Timothy when he shared this with him: "For the time will come when people will not put up with sound doctrine. Instead, to suit their own desires, they will gather around them a great number of teachers to say what their itching ear wants to hear" (2 Timothy 4:3 NIV). That time is here. Look around where you are and look at how communities are being affected by various doctrinal and religious teachings. There is a solid foundation that can hold together all communities if it is built on the solid word of God. Paul writes, "Nevertheless, God's solid foundation stands firm, sealed with this inscription: 'The Lord knows those who are his', and 'Everyone who confesses the name of the Lord must turn away from wickedness...And, let everyone that nameth the name of Christ depart from iniquity" (2 Timothy 2:19 NIV). There is a way to redeem oneself: repent. As John writes, "Repent of your sin, or I will come to you suddenly and fight against them with the sword of my mouth" (Revelation 2:16 NLT).

Thyatira

The fourth church is Thyatira. This church was too tolerant. There were no limitations and no boundaries. It was known as a trading outpost community. This community was permitting an openness of a lifestyle that went further than it should have. In everything, there must be limits, a time to say yeah or nay, but Thyatira was not this community. It reminds me of the story in the Old Testament when Moses went up into the mountains to hear from God, but he left Aaron with the congregation. The congregants who remained began to murmur and complain and wanted Aaron to allow them to be free—to tap into their wild side, if you will. This is what happens when you become too tolerant. As we read in Exodus,

When the people saw that Moses was so long in coming down from the mountain, they gathered around Aaron and said, "Come, make us gods who will go before us. As for this fellow Moses who brought us up out of Egypt, we don't know what has happened to him." (Exodus 32:1 NIV)

Moses was listening to and obeying God. In instances where people become restless and exhibit less patience, things can go awry in a community. The Lord further says to this church, "I know all the things you do. I have seen your love, your faith, your service, and your patient endurance. And I can see your constant improvement in all these things" (Revelation 2:19 NLT). Despite the good, there was a flaw: "You are permitting that woman—that Jezebel who calls herself a prophet—to lead my servants astray" (Revelation 2:20 NLT). Sometimes bad things outweigh the good, and "Therefore, do not let what you know is good be spoken of as evil" (Romans 14:16 NIV). Having the wrong person in the wrong place can set things back rather than move them forward in a community. There is only one way to put things back on track in the community went they go left: correct course and steer the ship in the right direction.

Sardis

The fifth church is Sardis. It's dead. There is no life, no example, no modeling of behavior to embrace. Its locality was fifty miles east of Smyrna, located on the southeast highway from Pergamum and Thyatira. It was also home to a large group of well-established Jews, called "Sephardic" after the city's name. John writes, "I know all the things you do, and that you have a reputation for being alive—but you are dead" (Revelation 3:1 NLT). What can be done in a community when it's dead

THE HEART OF MINISTRY

and there is no life? A spirit of lethargy will suck the life out of a community. A lack of enthusiasm and a tendency toward aimlessness bring frustration and heartache to all connected. What life was left was encouraged to keep moving. John writes, "Wake up! Strengthen what little remains for even what is left is almost dead" (Revelation 3:2). It appears from this text that the place was on life support. It barely existed. It was going down the wrong path and it was just a matter of time before the lights never turned on again. It's like that church in the community with the same five or six people who show up every week to hear the same presentations; the spirit of just existing surfaces in the room. Wake up! Stir up your pure mind and get a grip. The people who once lived in the community of Sardis were well-established Jews. This says a lot. There had to be people with many gifts and talents, experience, and wisdom, but it was dying.

As Paul writes to Timothy, "For this reason I remind you to fan into flame the gift of God, which is in you through the laying on of my hands" (2 Timothy 1:6 NIV). Paul saw something in Timothy he didn't see in himself. Many times, people in a community have so much potential and so much life to give. However, if no one is vigilant enough or vocal enough to call it out, nothing will ever become of the gift. It has been said the place with so many gifted people who never had the opportunity to use their talents is in the graveyard. Don't let your community die off. Don't let it go to ruins, and decay and fall. Rise up!

The most certain thing that will keep a community growing and expanding is never losing sight of the prize. The way you start is how you want to end. One of the most cited verses in this chapter about the church at Sardis is this: "Go back to what you believed and heard at first; hold to it firmly" (Revelation 3:3 NLT). That is powerful. Never losing hope, confidence, and the resilience to keep winning is what's needed to keep communities relevant and vibrant. Going back to a healthy start is not the same as moving backwards; it's just an opportunity to establish the footing that got you where you ended up in the first place. It was the drive, the energy, the love, the passion, and the dedication that took you to the next level. Somewhere along the way, you lost it. Getting back to basics is sometimes the only thing you need when things become unsettled. Let it work in your favor!

Philadelphia

The sixth church is Philadelphia. This church is weak but obedient. John writes, "I know all the things you do, and I have opened a door for you that no one can close. You have a little strength, yet you obeyed my word and did not deny me" (Revelation 3:8 NLT). John writes about an open door. This sounds like the mayor of a city giving someone a key to the city. Having a key to the city comes with rights and privileges that anyone would gladly accept. Access is necessary to maintaining, operating, and functioning well in a city environment. Another relevant point of having access to a community is knowing all the ins and outs of the city. There are so many things to learn about the services, outreach, and the day-to-day handling of affairs that are needed to help people get along.

One community had a very well-established business in it for years. The business continued to stay the course and remain constant even during obvious change. Suddenly, it became a victim of its environment. The services this business offered were office supplies, school supplies, office furnishings, copying services, shipping, and more. A person in the community had a vision to one day open her own copying service. The drive that motivated this person began to reflect the good the established business once offered its community. Despite the closing, the services were still needed. An open door was needed. God opened a door for this person. She began to put into place some of the very tools and services the former business had offered.

People came into her business sharing with her how glad they were for her opening in the community. The services they once enjoyed had come back to where it all began. The new owner in the community is standing and maintaining. It takes time for anything new to take off, but it goes back to knowing the ins and outs of a community and what services are needed. Community leaders need vision. As we read in Proverbs, "Where there is no revelation, people cast off restraint, but blessed is the one who heeds wisdom's instruction" (Proverbs 29:18 NIV).

One of the most painful experiences is traveling in a neighborhood aimlessly. This only contributes to losing time and not redeeming and valuing the time dedicated to a meaningful and purposeful call. When there are issues that seemingly throw a wrench into the plans of a new development or a new project in your community, don't quit! As it says in Proverbs, "If you falter in a time of trouble, how small is your strength!" (Proverbs 24:10 NIV). All is not lost. Perhaps this will give you a chance for a stronger return, better ideas, or a more direct, focused plan that will be just what the community needs. This church had opportunities coming towards them. Open doors don't come easily. When the door is opened, walk into the right one. Every door is not for you to enter. You will know if it's the right one. A community has the right person in the right place with the right plan to navigate you to your purpose.

Notwithstanding, this church had some weaknesses. There are weaknesses in a community that can contribute to things being delayed, not fulfilled, or not accomplished. Let's be clear: the human side of us doesn't always get things right the first time. If you are not careful, a weakness can abort your future, but you must have the resolve to press forward. As Paul writes, "But he said to me, 'My grace is sufficient for you, for my power is made perfect in weakness. Therefore, I will boast all the more gladly about my weaknesses, so that Christ's power may rest on me'" (2 Corinthians 12:9 NIV). This is a powerful way to see a weakness that may surface in a community. It is not over until God says it's over. Simply go back to the drawing board and surround yourself with people who can help you achieve the goal. More importantly, be willing to admit when you need assistance, help, or someone to come alongside you to make the task better. You don't wallow or sulk in the fault; you find the strength and tenacity to overcome it and see what you need to make it stronger.

Laodicea

The seventh church is Laodicea, which is styled as a lukewarm church and uncommitted. The writer writes, "I know all the things you do that you are neither hot nor cold. I wish that you were one or the other! But since you are lukewarm water, neither hot nor cold, I will spit you out of my mouth!" (Revelation 3:15–16 NLT). A church in a community with this attitude has no fire or vision to accomplish a work. You are either on or off. You either want to get something done or you don't. It takes focus, a plan, and a design to get through the halls of government. Unfortunately, this community didn't see its faults. We read, "You say, 'I am rich. I have everything I want. I don't need a thing!' And you don't realize that you are wretched and miserable and poor and blind and naked" (Revelation 3:17 NLT). There is only one outcome of a community out of touch with reality: a great fall. Businesses will pull out, families will leave the community, buildings will be boarded up, and the landscape will become unattended. The difference to turning this problem around is taking a good self-assessment of where you are in a community and making the necessary changes to win.

Making the necessary changes looks something like this. Suppose the church has had the same fixtures in its building from conception. The carpet is unraveling, the seating is stained, legs are getting weak, and the fixtures are dated, and it seems to not bother a soul. To continue this picture of this church in the community, there is no growth, no increase. The last thing you want to do is become stagnant, out of touch with reality, and with a nonchalant attitude. As this church failed to see it needed to do something different, it became a problem in the eyes of Christ. The church in a community is the representative of Jesus Christ. As we read in 1 Peter, "However, if you suffer as a Christian, do not be ashamed, but praise God that you bear that name" (1 Peter 4:16 NIV). The world is looking for a light, an example, a church with a good name. Communities want to be known for the good things they are doing, the strong programs they have instituted, and for having a heart and compassion for the people they serve.

Personal Reflection

My analysis has certainly given me a greater awareness and passion for the work I do as a pastoral counselor. Community is here to stay, and needs men and women who have a burden and concern for the people when major life-changing incidents and crises arise. Nehemiah has had a great impact on how I pursue situations that seem devastating. Nehemiah's heart was touched by the condition of the walls left in ruin in Jerusalem. The walls that have been destroyed or removed in today's communities need a Nehemiah to seek support or intervene on behalf of those communities. My research is bringing more focus for my future as a pastor and what health care services our church can provide. One of the unique ministries is our wellness group, headed by a very astute and caring leader. She holds a master's degree in public health. The leader of this group addresses various health awareness issues each month, including health screenings, health fairs, and mental health training. This is open to the community. The wellness manager shared these words.

The church still represents a valued infrastructure within the community. Having a wellness ministry in the church allows health promotion from a holistic approach (body, mind, spirit); it serves the members and the community. Providing more community health screenings, educational sessions, physical activities, and support services, particularly mental health, would be positive expansion strategies.

The pastoral counseling I provide as a pastor is free. I am not a licensed counselor. I willingly utilize the skills and training I have gained from all the education I have been afforded. I am an advocate for mental health and a certified mental health coach through the American Association of Christian Counselors. I can see things lining up better for me once I retire from my secular job in government. I ultimately want to participate in the heart of ministry. Giving my time, knowledge, and skills to this congregation and the people in the community will be an asset in whatever capacity God sees fit. A healthy congregation has a wide spectrum of many people with professional academic degrees to help make it better and more efficient. Our congregation has nurses, medical personnel, and mental health workers. In the past seven years, I have taken a great interest in pastoral counseling and pastoral care. The future of making a huge impact in the local community looks brighter every day.

Various facilities or institutions were once viable in the community to reach a mass audience of people, and the church is a mainstay. The church doors are always open to meet the needs of the people, even if it comes to mental health needs. A church provides meals, clothing, biblical knowledge, training, childcare, reading programs, and more. In this twenty-first century, in an ever-changing world, the church must be adaptable. A passage from the scripture reads, "Is there no balm in Gilead? Is there no physician there? Why then is there no healing for the wound of my people?" (Jeremiah 8:22, NIV). The effort to help bring an awareness of mental health issues is important. No one can take the mindset that "it is not my problem; it is someone else's problem."

I have shared my personal story of a tragedy I experienced as a child: my mother, at the age of twenty-nine, committed suicide. This devastated my life. I did not realize the impact her death had on me until I began to experience the deep loss of her nurturing and love. I had to battle my issue of mental depression. The thoughts of suicide ran rampant in my mind. It has been fifty years since my mom's passing. At the age of fifty-two, I came to the knowledge I suffered from undiagnosed post-traumatic stress disorder (PTSD) and never received the treatment I needed. The divine grace and healing from God covered my life.

My passion and heart are for the broken, wounded, and lost. When all players come together to reach a common goal, great things can happen. Miracles and blessings can take place. Where there is no vision, the people perish. I am grateful for the hope, compassion, and vision God has placed in us to do greater things in the communities we live in. The church is a beacon of light to a community. My role as the shepherd of the house carries a huge responsibility. The body of Christ needs to offer more than just music and preaching of the gospel dynamics in a ministry. Information, knowledge, effective programs, forums for discussion, and sharing of the heart and mind are all part of what a church should look like in the community. Some needs will be impossible to fulfill. In a fast-paced and changing climate, the question that needs to be addressed or the analysis that needs to occur is right before us. The community needs caring people with hearts to make a difference. I want to take up this mantle and be part of the change. To see a change, you must become the change you want to see.

Introduction

Strategies for Processes in Ministry

The work of a ministry is designed with the right people leading at the helm of the work of God. It is clearly mapped; the organizational hierarchy is presented and given to us as the model to live by. As we read in Ephesians, "And he gave some to be apostles, some prophets, some evangelists, some pastors, and teachers, equipping the saints for the work of ministry, to build up the body of Christ" (Ephesians 4:11–12). All these layers have one purpose: ensuring the processes in place are working in sync for the betterment of all of those in a ministry. Note that there are only five. God is smart enough to know what is needed for effective ministry processes. The five-fold ministry is a great start to address the spiritual growth and development of the church and its congregation. A growing church is a thriving church, and there is more to come as it develops and matures in the grace of God. It is clearly understood everyone does not have the same purpose. Some is key as this book heighten information prepared for your learning. Some is defined as "at least a small amount or number of people or things." It is amazing how the least number of roles that have been carefully and adeptly written in the word of God for the purpose of the ministry to succeed can accomplish its design. It is not a broken process; it is one that must be exercised by those who take on this work for the glory and honor of God.

Processes meet intended purposes or goals in an organization. The left hand must know what the right hand is doing for everyone connected to be going in the same direction. As stated in Proverbs, "Plans fail for lack of counsel, but with many advisers they succeed" (Proverbs 15:22 NIV). There needs to be an equipping of the saints to help them achieve the goals and expectations required of them to lead, guide, and perform. To show up for work in a ministry is one thing, but coming well-prepared, organized, and equipped sets the stage for total success. An implementation map is an idea to develop a path to reach a destiny in the work of ministry. One of the greatest shepherds in the Bible is David. He had one simple expression for leading people: "He leadeth me beside still waters...He leadeth me in the paths of righteousness" (Psalm 23:2–3).

The ministry of Jesus produced a model blueprint for the development and assignment of men and women in ministry. There is a world waiting for someone to lead the charge and establish the path to success. As Matthew writes, "Therefore, go and make disciples of all nations, baptizing them in the name of the Father, and of the Son and of the Holy Spirit and teaching them to obey everything I have commanded you. And surely, I am with you, always, to the very end of the age" (Matthew 28:20). A disciple is a follower of Christ. One must be taught, trained, and prepared for the call God places on that person to work the ministry he has appointed him or her to do.

Church Resources

What tools and resources are needed to move an organization from point A to point B? It must be understood that one of the most valuable resources in ministry is people. People are necessary and essential for work to get off the ground. Churches need people of all ages, background experiences, and education. As the work, roles, and resources are identified, everything begins to come together like clockwork. Resources provide training, and a learning environment affords the opportunity to make assessments of the strengths and weaknesses of an organization. For the knowledge and wisdom gained in learning, leaders must be empowered. The people a leader has trained are given an opportunity to shine.

The ant is a powerful example of how to move people toward progress. In Proverbs, we read, "Go to the ant, thou sluggard, consider her ways, and be wise: which having no guide, overseer, or ruler, provideth her meat in the summer, and gathereth her food in the harvest" (Proverbs 6:6–8). What do you see happening in this scenario? You see one of the tiniest creatures on earth serving as the model of working in the right season preparing for the next season. There is initiative, there is drive, and there is focus on all happening in real time without having to be watched, instructed, or told. The ant exercises survival skills. A rainy day is coming in all our lives. An organization will encounter highs and lows, and profits and losses, but you can't just sit there and do nothing. As we read in Ecclesiastes, "Whatever your hand finds to do, do it with all your might, for in the realm of the dead, where you are going, there is neither working nor planning nor knowledge nor wisdom" (Ecclesiastes 9:10 NIV).

Let's take a view of the processes Moses established when the house of the Lord was being built. Remember, the greatest asset or resource for an organization is the people. From Exodus, we know that "Bezalel, Oholiab, and all the skilled people are to work based on everything the Lord has commanded. The Lord has given them wisdom and understanding to know how to do all the work of constructing the sanctuary" (Exodus 36:1 NIV). It takes skills and giftings to put forth an effort that will glorify God. Individuals will pursue their academic success by attending a two-year or four-year college in a major that wins their hearts. The sacrifice, the hours of study, and the late night reading and preparation for exams has an end game down the line. Once you begin, it must be a hearty moment to finish what you started. As we read in Exodus, "So Moses summoned Bezalel, Oholiab, and every skilled person in whose heart the Lord had placed wisdom., all whose hearts moved them, to come to the work and do it" (Exodus 36:2 NIV). Processes are fully exemplified for what's about to start. Are you available and reliable to put skin in the game for a winning combination?

Characteristics of a Thriving Congregation

Introduction

The early church from the book of Acts was successful and growing because of one experience: the birthing and outpouring of the Holy Spirit. The message of the gospel of Jesus Christ captured the minds and lives of all of those who were introduced to the wonderful saving grace of our Lord and Savior, Jesus Christ, the son of the living God. This process resulted from obedience and waiting on the promise of God.

The scriptures revealed the way the Holy Spirit would come. Acts 1:4–5 states, "And being assembled together with them, He commanded them not to depart from Jerusalem, but to wait for the Promise of the Father, 'which' He said, 'you have heard from Me; for John truly baptized with water, but you shall be baptized with the Holy Spirit not many days from now.'" The days of waiting and seeking the power and anointing of the Holy Spirit would change their lives forever. The Spirit came to give direction, knowledge, and, more important, power. "But you shall receive power when the Holy Spirit has come upon you; and you shall be witnesses to Me, in Jerusalen, and in all Judea and Samaria, and to the end of the earth." Let's unwrap this moment. Power is not about ruling or being forceful; it is having the authority and boldness to represent the witness that has been placed in you. The power provides the confidence, assurance, and willingness to share the gospel of Jesus Christ, which is what changes lives. You may ask, "How can the congregation I'm serving become the congregation God wants it to become?" The answer is in Zechariah: "So, he answered and said to me: This is the word of the Lord to Zerubbabel: Not by might nor by power, but by my Spirit, Says the Lord of hosts" (Zechariah 4:6).

An individual must have something inside of him or her to be an effective witness. Until the power is in you, stay in place and be empowered for it to come. A thriving church needs thriving people. People who understand their assignments and the means and processes that will take a congregation to the level God wants it to go require the Spirit of God taking the lead.

The Witness to Lead

How does one prepare himself or herself to take the lead of a powerful and growing organization? How does the witness inside of that person rise for the occasion to take the world by storm? Boldness! Boldness births the fire and energy to set the course of the world on fire. The wrong spirit entering a situation will take a ministry in the wrong direction. In James, we read, "The tongue also is a fire, a world of evil among the parts of the body. It corrupts the whole person, sets the whole course of his life on fire, and is itself set on fire by hell" (James 3:6). A wise and engaged leader recognizes when a matter of the heart is going in the wrong path. He or she takes the authority to bring the work in line with its intended purpose, to make a difference in people's lives.

The witness born in you is to bring forth good fruit, good vibes, good evidence, and great results. Peter had to take the leadership of bringing a thriving church together. He stood up and made his voice heard on high:

And with many words he testified and exhorted them, saying, "Be saved from this perverse generation." Then those who gladly received his word were baptized; and that day about three thousand souls were added to them. And they continued steadfastly in the apostles' doctrine and fellowship, in the breaking of bread, and in prayers." (Acts 2:40–41)

There was an expectation for the church to have a great impact in the community. A community-focused ministry takes into consideration everyone who tries to enter the doors of the church. Their needs are what matters, their concerns are important, and their voices need to be heard. The Spirit of God moved mightily and, as a result, the church grew exponentially. Coming together to know the way of living for Christ brought about a change in their behavior. As noted in Acts, "Then fear came upon every soul, and many wonders and signs were done through the apostles" (Acts 2:43). A reverence for God will always bring a level of honor and respect unlike any other power. It doesn't matter what degrees you have on your wall or how many letters are behind your name. Without the Spirit and presence of God reigning in your heart, these do not matter. The result is having the drive, tenacity, and skillset to bring the right leader to take the wheel.

There will be moments of trial and setbacks to come against leading a thriving church. In that moment a word of encouragement will drop your way: "Why did the nations rage, and the people plot vain things? The kings of the earth took their stand, and the rulers were gathered together against the Lord and against His Christ" (Acts 4:25). Through all this, the courage to stand, press onward, and press through shined in the lives of these bold leaders. That's what happens to you. You will speak loudly, boldly, and directly into the enemy of the soul. Acts tells us,

"Now Lord, look on their threats, and grant to your servants that with all boldness they may speak your word, by stretching your hand to heal, and that signs and wonders may be done through the name of Your holy Servant Jesus" (Acts 4:29).

Strength Made Perfect in Weakness

Let's be honest. In a thriving and growing ministry, there are moments when the trying of your faith takes place. The human factor takes a toil on every leader or person who has a role in serving a ministry. It takes an honest assessment to acknowledge and recognize an individual's strengths and weaknesses that surface in serving. The apostle Paul knew firsthand the reality of facing the challenges and setbacks that crossed his path. An infirmity or a thorn was a concern in Paul's life. He sought God through prayer three times for the problem to be removed. How many of us seek God in prayer to deliver us out of a worrisome personal trial or situation? This was Paul's Achilles' heel. It didn't go away. Leaders, there will be problems in ministry that you want to go away but, for some good reason, will not. Let's park right here and read from Romans: "We know that all good things work together for the good of those who love God, who are called according to his purpose" (Romans 8:28). The setback in your thriving congregation has a purpose. Something in this moment is to make greater things and experiences to come. Your greatest defeat can become your most triumphant moment.

The best way to make it in a season of challenges is to accept what the will of the Lord is for your life. As Paul writes,

> Therefore, so that I would not exalt myself, a thorn in the flesh was given to me, a messenger of Satan to torment me so that I would not exalt myself. Concerning this, I pleaded with the Lord

three times that it would leave me. But he said to me, "My grace is sufficient for you, for my power is perfected in weakness." (2 Corinthians 12:7–9)

That was the answer given to Paul. The same answer given to him stands in play for you as well. Never look at a weakness as an insufficiency in you: it is never about you. It is always what's the best decision, the best move, or the best strategy for the work of the ministry you are leading and serving. This further keeps humility in the forefront of it all. What was one of the attributes that made Jesus's ministry unlike any other? It was his humility. Paul writes,

> But made of himself no reputation, and took upon him the form of a servant, and was made in the likeness of men: And being found in fashion as a man, he humbled himself, and became obedient unto death, even the death of the cross. Wherefore God also hath highly exalted him and given him a name which is above every name: That at the name of Jesus, every knee should bow, of things in heaven, and things in earth, and things under the earth." (Philippians 2:7–10)

Faith sharing is a must to condition the hearts of followers of Christ. In times of trouble, uncertainty, challenges, and obstacles that seek to derail a church that has been a pillar in the community for years, one must never give up hope. Tomorrow is not promised but you can't allow the present to abort what lies ahead for the future. The Bible verse in Psalm covers a moment of frailty and distress: "My times are in your hands; deliver me from the hands of the enemies, from those who pursue me" (Psalm 31:15).

Congregational Sustainability

Introduction

The sustainability of a ministry has its own set of twists, turns, and bumps in the road. Sustainability is meeting our own needs without compromising the ability of future generations to meet their own needs. In a previous chapter, I mentioned the seven churches that were part of their various communities, some in good ways and others not so good. In discussing the sustainability of congregations, one of those churches is a good point of reference to bring into this conversation. The letter to the church in Philadelphia states, "I know your works. Look. I have placed before you an open door that no one can close because you have but little power; yet you have kept my word and have not denied my name" (Revelations 3:8). The endurance and perseverance this church modeled kept them in good standing with God. It wasn't known for its popularity or its strong presence, but the little power and presence it had touched the heart of God.

A congregation with a reverence and respect for God can stand the test of time. God sees and knows the heart of humankind and he knows if motives are genuine or not; it is in that moment he will open doors that no person can shut. When others count you out, you will rise, and they will be looking up to you and wondering how you got here. A sustaining church will not be lacking or slacking, but "the Lord will perfect that which concerns me" (Psalm 138:8). That's a sustainable church. The church in Philadelphia kept something that is important for ministry. Let the church be the church and let the focus and intent of the church be the consistent factor for its sustainability: adhering to the word of God. The psalmist David understood this quite well: "Thy word have I hid in my heart that I might not sin against thee" (Psalm 119:11). The favor of God will give you the strength, might, and will to hold on in spite the various challenges, delays, and problems that will arise. Every ministry will face hard times, valley days, mountain days, and even glory days. The blessing is staying the course through them all. Your faithfulness, consistency, determination, and drive make the difference. This church had a crown coming and no one on earth could take it away.

A must have for the sustainability of a congregation is having a faith in God that will not be moved. In the words of Hebrews, "Faith is confidence in what we hope for and assurance about what we do not see" (Hebrews 11:1).

A Steady Race

The life of a runner requires strength training, endurance training, maintaining a healthy diet, and managing good weight practices. The applicable training doesn't happen with just one occurrence. There is a continual process of meeting the physical demands for the sole purpose of winning a race. The training also requires good rest and being emotionally healthy for the task at hand. These disciplines alone will bring forth much-needed good fruit while in a race serving God. In the writings of Paul, he appears to understand a lot about racing.

The witnesses that surround one in ministry are treasured resources for learning the when, where, and how of what needs to be done to keep it going and successful. Those before you have done the necessary heavy lifting to prepare the way for success and many valuable opportunities. As we read in Hebrews, "Therefore, since we are surrounded by such a great cloud of witnesses, let us throw off everything that hinders and the sin that so easily entangles. And let us run with perseverance the race marked for us" (Hebrews 12:1). Is there something in your life in ministry you need to take off or remove? Are there sinful habits that are unbecoming in a Christian's walk with God? To stay on the course and win the race takes a well-disciplined and focused mindset. Sin can entangle you and bring about hindrances that cause setbacks or failure. As we read in Ephesians, "But among you there must not be even a hint of sexual immorality, or any kind of impurity, or of greed, because these are improper for God's holy people" (Ephesians 5:3). Today several men in ministry have succumbed to falls. They did not have accountability, boundaries, and other valuable resources in their toolkits to avoid such occurrence. It is important to keep the main thing the main thing. Sustainability also requires steadfastness to remain committed and faithful to your responsibilities without yielding to distractions to pull you away from the task. As Paul writes, "Therefore, my dear brothers and sisters, stand firm. Let nothing move you. Always give yourselves fully to the work of the Lord because you know that your labor in the Lord is not in vain" (1 Corinthians 15:58).

In closing, your sustainability determines just how far you will go in ministry. Preparation makes the difference for what lies ahead. A leader will be tested and tried, and may even come to a place of wanting to give up. Paul writes, "Each one's work will become clear; for the Day will declare it, because it will be revealed by fire; and the fire will test each one's work, of what worth it is. If anyone's work which he has built on it endures, he will receive a reward" (1 Corinthians 3:14). Stay the course! It's worth it.

A Disciplined Body

I indicated earlier that Paul could have possibly been involved in foot racing. He uses the analogy of running races, winning, endurance, and patience. Yes, it takes discipline and patience to stay in a race. This leads to disciplining the body. The training mentioned in the previous chapter laid out what it takes to be sustainable. Let's examine the words of Paul: "Don't you realize that in a race everyone runs, but only one person gets the prize?" So run to win!" (1 Corinthians 9:24). Many people strive and hope to win the prize. Some prepare themselves more, condition themselves more, and take their bodies seriously. In the same way, leaders and servants in ministry must conduct our lives in a way to ensure a win. Only one will be the ultimate winner, but it does not take anything away from you taking the approach as a winner in all you do.

Paul further expounds on something bigger than a physical race. In having a disciplined body, one must also have a disciplined mind. As a man thinketh, so is he. Paul writes, "All athletes are disciplined in their training. They do it to win a prize that will fade away, but we do it for an eternal prize" (1 Corinthians 9:25). The spiritual value outweighs the natural value. Eternal life is the goal for winning this race. One must have a purpose and a vision to achieve the things wanted and desired in ministry. Endurance will produce the sustainability and faith to conquer whatever the mind is set to do.

The question at hand is how effective is and what is the benefit of a disciplined body? What is the long-term benefit for an organization with established processes and people adhering and cooperating? It is quite simple. Profits and gains are wanted in an organization; that's about winning and not losing. The spiritual insight leads to this assessment: "For physical training is of some value, but godliness has value for all things, holding promise for both the present life and the life to come" (1 Timothy 4:8) The

THE HEART OF MINISTRY

ultimate objective in the whole scheme of things is to demonstrate godliness in all you do. Godliness sustains you, protects you, and, more importantly, keeps you moving in the right direction.

A disciplined body further requires a healthy body. A healthy congregation brings forth the right fruit needed to grow and flourish. There is a lot of discussion concerning self-care. Self-care is essential to alleviate burnout and stress that can happen in ministry with pastors. It is a healthy thing to find time for exercise. Find an activity to step away from the busyness and burden that comes along with serving a congregation. As Paul writes, "For physical training is of some value, but godliness has value for all things, holding promise for both the present life and the life to come" (1 Timothy 4:8). Physical conditioning adds a great impact in managing the day-to-days tasks that come with the roles serving the Lord. The current crisis of a pandemic has added anxiety, depression, uncertainty, and more. Make self-care part of your life. Self-care is not selfish. God wants you to live your best life. He wants you to live a healthy life, to "enjoy good health and that all may go well with you, even as your soul is getting along well" (3 John 1:2).

Organizational Fit with Congregational Needs

Introduction

Organizational fit is vitally important to ensure the mission and purpose of the work is aligned and equipped with all the dynamics needed for a smooth operation. A candidate should have a personal set of work values that align well with the established norms of the company's organizational structure. What are the work values you possess? Are you dependable, reliable, and accessible? It is within reason that your availability is considered with other things going on in one's life. At the end of the day, the mission and the ministry must survive and remain sustainable. If the organization is in the right fit, the needs of the congregation will be job one. The needs and guidance, direction, and focus will ensure the ship is being steered in the right direction.

In examining the needs of a congregation, first understand why the members of a church are there. The early church in the book of Acts was a church that had all things in common. The needs of the people were met accordingly as they shared and engaged with one another, with spirituality at the forefront of their gatherings. A community needs to feel a church in their vicinity is meeting a need for their families, their children, and their lives. When this happens, the church will grow. As we read in Hebrews, "And let us consider how we may spur one another toward love and good deeds, not giving up meeting together, as some are in the habit of doing, but encouraging one another-and all the more as you see the Day approaching" (Hebrews 10:24–25).

Fit to Serve

Daniel is a great example in the Bible that depicts what the right fit looks like for an organization and a congregation. Daniel was not seeking to fit in with the culture he was living in during his time in leadership; he stood for what he knew was right. He didn't compromise his faith, his biblical teaching, or his ethics. Daniel had the opportunity to eat the finest of food and drink the best wine, but he chose not to do it. Something stood up in him to display the heart and character of a man who didn't want to fit in the house of the king. The house he wanted to abide in was the house of the Lord in his own heart. He made his body a living sacrifice unto the Lord. As Paul later iterated, "Do you not know that your bodies are temples of the Holy Spirit, who is in you, whom you have received from God? You are not your own; you were bought with a price. Therefore, honor God with your bodies" (1 Corinthians 6:19–20). Daniel's love for God was evident in his walk with him. Our walk should align with the word of God; this ensures blessing in all you do. Ethics is a must to have in place for organizational structure. Let's explore more about the character of Daniel.

We read that "Daniel so distinguished himself among the administrators and satraps by his exceptional qualities that the king planned to set him over the whole kingdom" (Daniel 6:3). That's awesome! When the right man's or woman's skills and abilities are recognized by those in authority, they better know what to do with what they see. Don't miss out on the opportunity to thrive, excel, and soar when these people come into your life.

There will be moments when the next best enters your world. Perhaps they are present for the moment after seeking God in prayer for roles and positions to be filled. Never rely on the skillset of one person and assume he or she can multitask. You will eventually be let down because putting too much responsibility on one person leads to burnout. Achieving balance and spreading the wealth of knowledge are the right moves. Make the playing field level.

The Congregational Needs

In demonstrating a good fit in an organization, one must set the guidelines and boundaries that should be respected and followed. Organizations need strong and solid financial structures to keep the business flowing. The organization needs accountability and someone steering the ship in the right direction. The servant known as Joshua loved God and his family, and he loved the assignment that was on his life. These words convey the ultimate essence of one defending and protecting the place he has been given authority over. Joshua's faith was committed to God so strongly that he used his faith to cover his household. Men serve as the heads of their households. In leading and serving our families, this same mindset carries into the house of God. A congregation needs a leader who will protect, guide, lead, and provide sound wisdom and instruction. In the book of Joshua, we read,

> But if serving the Lord seems undesirable to you, then choose for yourselves this day whom you will serve, whether the gods your ancestors served beyond the Euphrates, or the gods of the Amorites, in whose land you are living. But as for me and my household, we will serve the Lord. (Joshua 24:15)

That's a declarative statement; indeed, my house will serve the Lord. Can you see the clarity, the directness, and the thoroughness of this decision? It is without question that everyone has his or her own opinion or own self-interest as it pertains to matters of the heart.

There is only *one* and true and living God, not those little gods that can lead one astray or away from the purpose of life. Pastors who serve ministries today declare to the congregation the one who should be exalted above all others. Psalm 40 says,

> I have proclaimed glad tidings of righteousness in the great congregation; Behold I will not restrain my lips, O Lord, You Know. I have not hidden Your righteousness within my heart; I have spoken of Your faithfulness and Your salvation; I have not concealed Your lovingkindness and Your truth from the great congregation. (Psalm 40:9–10)

In closing, a person's need for connection is essential to a sense of ownership of serving in a congregation. There are many hours given to serve in ministry. An investment of your skills and talents is willingly offered to a church as a volunteer not on payroll. God's love and his presence, warmth, and kindness should change the thermostat in the room. As Paul writes, "Therefore, as we have opportunity, let us do good to all people, especially to those who belong to the family of believers" (Galatians 6:10). Make the connection count.

Congregational Learning and Congregational Life

Introduction

The scriptures reveal the life of one of the greatest prophets who ever lived: John the Baptist. John was a forerunner of Christ who was preparing the way for his masterful introduction to the world. We read, "There was a man sent from God whose name was John. This man came for a witness, to bear witness of the Light, that all through him might believe. He was not that Light but was sent to bear witness of that Light" (John 1:6–8). His purpose was to prepare the way for the Savior of the world. His voice was powerful; it was a voice of revelation educating the people in his presence of this soul-stirring announcement: "I am the voice of one crying in the wilderness: Make straight the way of the Lord" (John 1:23).

A congregation's openness and passion to know about Christ is the ultimate purpose of those who gather in the audience. A congregation must be teachable and eager to know the ways of the Lord, and to become good stewards, good families, good husbands, wives, and good people. Learning is a continuous process. There are those who seek to learn but only to grasp its richness and wholesomeness; they are "always learning but never able to come to a knowledge of the truth" (2 Timothy 3:37). How can this be changed? This can be changed by getting to know the real purpose of congregational life. Enjoy the journey of learning as a student of the word of God. Isaiah states, "The Sovereign Lord has given me a well-instructed tongue, to know the word that sustains the weary. He awakens me morning by morning, wakens my ear to listen like one being instructed" (Isaiah 50:4).

A Skilled Congregation

Today's congregations flourish with fresh, vibrant, and engaged men and women across the spectrum. Young people are now joining in the forces of ministry, using their computer tech skills to produce promotional ads with smart apps, using videography for recording church services, and more. A thriving congregation is moving on the fast track to keeping up with what's around them. The last place a congregation wants to be is behind the times in the world we live in. If there ever was a time for the sons of Issachar to rise in a congregation with their needed skills, it is *now*. In 1 Chronicles, we read, "From Issachar, men who understood the times and knew what Israel should do—200 chiefs, with all their relatives under their command" (1 Chronicles 12:32). It takes skills and resourcefulness to manage a ministry well. The work of the church must be equipped with the minds and intelligence of sons and daughters who have the available tools and resources to keep it moving. Never be afraid of implementing new ways and tools to raise the bar of sharing the gospel of Jesus Christ. Many churches today are using flat screens, digital projectors, lights, and more to enhance the presentation of their ministries. The main objective is to bring glory and honor to God. Psalm 19 says, "The heavens are telling of the glory of God; And their expanse is declaring the work of His hands" (Psalm 19:1).

A powerful proverb comes to mind when considering

movement in a ministry: "Go to the ant, you sluggard; consider its ways and be wise! It has no commander, no overseer, or ruler, yet it stores its provisions in summer and gathers its food at harvest" (Proverbs 6:6–8). There is a real lesson to be learned from one of the smallest creatures on earth. An ant prepares for what's coming. It doesn't wait to be told what or how to do. It doesn't need to be reminded of an activity. It has a proactive approach to take care of business by any means necessary. The ant is bearing wisdom. As Proverbs reminds us, "Get wisdom, get understanding: forget it not; neither decline from the words of my mouth. Forsake her not, and she shall preserve thee: love her, and she shall keep thee. Wisdom is the principal thing; therefore, get wisdom: and with all thy wisdom get understanding" (Proverbs 4:5–7).

An Informed Congregation

Congregations are bodies of people that make up the household of faith. This includes elders, ministers, deacons, laity, apostles, evangelists, women in ministry, and more. These people carry out the tasks and functions of the church in a manner that brings glory and honor to God. A congregation should have a focused heart to win souls to Christ. The role of a pastor is to teach, preach, and feed the congregation for their growth in the Lord. Three things will happen when a clear understanding of the role of God's servant as a shepherd is manifested among the people. The shepherd is here, as stated in scripture, "for the perfecting of the saints, for the work of the ministry, for the edifying of the body of Christ" (Ephesians 4:12). The functioning of an informed congregation is taking place right here.

The atmosphere of a congregation should be one that offers engaged and focused learning. The resources used, the books, the technology, the lessons, and the preached word all have their place to ensure those in attendance are being fed. Philip, an evangelist in the Bible, helped a young man who was riding in a chariot reading the word of God. In his reading, the comprehension was not clear. He writes, "Then the Spirit said to Philip, 'Go near and overtake this chariot.' So, Philip ran to him, and heard him reading the prophet Isaiah, and said, 'Do you understand what you are reading?' And he said, 'How can I, unless someone guides me?'" (Acts 8:29–31) Guidance is necessary for congregational development and growth. Just as Phillip assisted the eunuch, God has placed shepherds to do the same. As we read in Jeremiah, "Then I will give you shepherds after my own heart, who will lead you with knowledge and understanding" (Jeremiah 3:15). Make the most of the opportunity to make a difference in the lives of those you serve.

What happens when the environment of learning or growth of a congregation is not provided? Insight, knowledge, and sharing of knowledge makes a congregation strong and viable. As we read in Hosea, "My people are destroyed from lack of knowledge. "Because you have rejected knowledge, I also reject you as my priests; because you have ignored the law of your God, I also will ignore your children" (Hosea 4:6). Knowledge is power. In our present world, the crisis of a global pandemic has impacted our country in a manner no one could have ever imagined. The coronavirus hit the world and lives began to be lost, families suffered great losses, grief, heartache, and panic. The media shared the loss of life daily in real-time with the demographics where the virus was strongly impacting individuals. Medical professionals were hard hit, working even to the point of exhaustion. The purpose of all the information was to inform people of what was taking place on the ground. Just as the world was being informed to protect the people, the same energy is directed in ministry. Saving lives is not about your political affiliation, socio-economic status, or your racial identity; it is for the love and concern of all humanity. Where should someone find help and good information in a time of need or a crisis? The church! Many issues are happening in the lives of the people who gather in a house of worship. It is not the role of the pastor of a congregation to make decisions for those he or she serves. However, the pastor should inform the congregation of issues that can impact their lives as well as their families' lives.

One notable moment was after scientists developed a vaccine. This vaccine became a subject in many family households. Fear and acceptance of the vaccine took center stage. When a congregation is alarmed, the voice of the shepherd needs to be heard to bring calm to alleviate fear and the risk of harm. The president of the United States employed pastors and churches to helping spread the vaccine message. Members of congregations looked to their churches to provide counsel and requested letters to submit to their employers when vaccinations became mandatory. How many of you know there is nothing new under the sun and the word of God can speak to a world's crisis? In my own personal experience, I found myself seeking to inform persons who sought my counsel about the vaccination. This passage of scripture was my reference point: "One person considers one day more sacred than another; another considers every day alike. Each of them should be fully convinced in their own mind" (Romans 14:5). An informed congregation receives information; the choices they make are up to them.

Introduction

The Importance of Leadership Management

The organizational management and processes that enable everyday administrative, leadership, and financial activities are relevant and vital for the success, good discipline, and order of a church organization. The biblical verse "Let all things be done decently and in order" (1 Corinthians 14:40) includes just what it states: "all things." The house of God should be the model entity in a community. It should handle its affairs in a manner that reflects the light and love of Christ. The church's plans, agenda, and objectives must embrace the practice of doing things well and keeping all matters in good order. As a former military leader, two of the principles I embraced during my tenure in the Republic of Korea were good order and discipline. Many situations affected the lives of people in that environment. The only way the organization managed to survive was by the fine, strong, and disciplined leadership of the commander. Leaders in our churches lead the charge for excellence. A leader must lead with integrity, in excellence, and with the right spirit.

Taking the Right Steps in Ministry

Psalm 37 says, "The steps of a good man are ordered by the Lord and he delighteth in his way" (Psalm 37:23). In the following chapters, I provide examples of men and women leading the work of the church and utilizing their executive skills, knowledge, and experience to make it happen. There are many examples of administrative and executive roles performed and carried out in the word of God. These include the dynamic leadership of Nehemiah, who rebuilt a damaged wall in fifty-two days, and Deborah, a woman judge who led her group to a victorious win. It takes strength, courage, drive, and tenacity to accomplish the work of the Lord. When our hands are at the plows, it is with one purpose in mind. Execute well!

Leadership, Management, and Administration

Introduction

One of the most notable characters in the Bible who was skilled, talented, and anointed to serve in the field of administration is Joseph. Joseph's ability to take charge and handle the affairs of a kingdom garnered the attention of Pharaoh in the land of Egypt. He became the person to ensure the safety, guidance, and well-being of God's people. Joseph was a man full of discernment and wisdom, which was needed for the work at hand. Besides having the right skills and abilities, there was something else that was needed to complete the task at hand. As Genesis 41:37–38 states, "The proposal pleased Pharaoh and all his servants, and he said to them, 'Can we find anyone like this, a man who has God's spirit in him?'" Someone within the organization may be the right person to complete an assignment. It is in leadership and management that the person appointed for this task needs to stand above his or her peers, have the right stuff, and the intelligence, knowledge, and wisdom to create a win–win situation. The administration under Pharaoh knew who the right man for the work was. Therefore, "Pharaoh said to Joseph, 'Since God has made all this known to you, there is no one as discerning and wise as you are'" (Genesis 41:39). His giftedness further placed him in a key role to take full charge of the problem they were facing. Pharaoh charged Joseph, "You will be over my house, and all my people will obey your commands" (Genesis 41:40). The person with the administrative and leadership skills must be ready to step into the job on day one. In the New Testament, Luke advises,

> But the one who does not know and does things deserving punishment will be beaten with few blows. From everyone who has given much, much will be demanded; and from the one who has been entrusted with much, much more will be asked. (Luke 12:48 NIV)

The Ability to Take Charge

The church has one main mission: to encourage men and women to have life-changing experiences with Christ. This mission must be clearly defined and understood so that everyone connected to a ministry understands the work to be done. If an organization is not careful, it can easily lose its way and find itself doing what it is not designed to do. How does one stay on the course? How does one know the difference between formal and informal processes and protocol and how they help to determine effective church leadership, programs, and activities? The ministry must stay on task. Paul writes, "Now you are the body of Christ, and individual members of it. And God has appointed these in the church: first apostles, second prophets, third teachers, next miracles, then gifts of healing, helping, administrating, various kinds of tongues" (1 Corinthians 12:27–28). Following what is written will ensure the work of ministry is carried out as prescribed for doing the business of the Lord. It can never be about you. It always must be about God and what He wants done for the purpose of growing and enhancing the kingdom of God. Processes enable an organization to flow without delay or interruption. Knowing what a formal or informal process is will depend on the structure of the ministry. There is church polity, articles of corporation, and so on. Each ministry functions according to the guidelines and written rules of order to ensure there is a form of accountability and good order.

Gifting of Administration

It really should not be a surprise to discover the real work in ministry is conducted behind the scenes by skilled and knowledgeable men and women. An organization's success is predicated on having the required skillsets and experiences to accomplish its mission. The mission is to do the Lord's business in an excellent way. In the biblical times of Solomon building God a house, he wanted the best of materials, the best architects, the best masonry, and the list goes on and on. Jethro advised Moses to put skilled leaders, men who feared and reverenced God, and behaved rightly to conduct the affairs of the people he served. This leads to the gifting of administration.

Leadership administration is defined as orchestrating tasks, and often mobilizing people, to develop and sustain an organization. In 1 Corinthians, Paul focused on the gift of administration among several other gifts, writing, "And God has appointed in the church first of all apostles, second prophets, third teachers, then miracles, then gifts of healing, of helping, of guidance, and of different kinds of tongues" (1 Corinthians 12:28 NIV). Not everyone has the anointing to serve in this capacity. When the person shares his or her giftedness in administration, the organization will come to the top because of it. Roles of an organization are in place for a reason. Not all have the same roles. Therefore, roles are assigned according to individuals' hearts and talents.

Roles and Responsibilities

Introduction

The roles and responsibilities assigned to individuals are necessary and important for the growth and sustainability of an organization. Roles are the functions assumed or parts played by people or things in a particular situation. Responsibilities are things one is required to do as part of a job, role, or legal obligation. The church must execute the discipline of these characteristics to see activities carried out in an effective manner. The beauty of the roles and responsibilities in the church is that everyone should be focused on its kingdom purpose. It is never about an individual or a personality, or about the charisma that one may possess. When the focus is on the right target, the process of accomplishing the mission is minimized by fewer distractions. Paul writes, "According to the grace of God which is given unto me, as a wise master builder I have laid the foundation, and another buildeth theron. But let every man take heed how he buildeth thereupon" (1 Corinthians 3:10).

Three groups in ministry have weighted and valuable roles to keep the work of ministry flowing: elders, deacons, and pastors. These persons execute one common thread of oneness: the instructing and teaching of the word of God to a congregation.

The Office of a Bishop

Paul wrote the following about bishops.

> This is a faithful saying: if a man desires the position of a bishop, he desires a good work. A bishop then must be blameless, the husband of one wife, temperate, soberminded, of good behavior, hospitable, able to teach, not given to wine, not violent, not greedy for money, but gentle, not quarrelsome, not covetous; one who rules his own house well, having his children in submission with all reverence (for if a man does not know how to rule his own house, how will he take care of the church of God?), not a novice, lest being puffed up with pride he fall into the same condemnation as the devil." (1 Timothy 3:1–6)

This role is executed with a good moral compass. The man or woman who steps into this place of leadership has a clearly defined job description that should not be overlooked. Bishops should have wise counsel, conduct sincere prayer and fasting, and seek for the assurance that the congregation heard the right word. They should preach the gospel and go into a room somewhere and pray.

The Qualifications of Deacons

Likewise, deacons must be reverent, not double-tongued, not given to much wine, not greedy for money, and hold the mystery of the faith with a pure conscience. Let these also first be tested; then, if found blameless, let them serve as deacons. Likewise, their wives must be reverent, temperate, faithful in all things, and not slanderers. Let a deacon be the husband of one wife, ruling their children and their own houses well. For those who have served well as deacons obtain for themselves a good standing and great boldness in the faith which in Christ Jesus" (1 Timothy 3:8–13). Another clear and well-defined role in the church is the work of a deacon. How does one go about being proven? What is the test to determine if one called to serve as a deacon is ready to take on the work? In the end, a deacon is a servant, one who gives of himself or herself to others to make the work of ministry move along effectively.

Qualified Elders

Titus 1:5–9 states,

> For this reason I left you in Crete, that you should set in order the things that are lacking and appoint elders in every city as I commanded you. If a man is blameless, the husband of one wife, having faithful children not accused of dissipation or insubordination. For a bishop must be blameless, as a steward of God, not self-willed, not quick-tempered, not given to wine, not violent, not greedy for money, but hospitable, a lover of what is good, sober-minded, just, holy, self-controlled, holding fast the faithful word as he has been taught, that he may be able, by sound doctrine, both to exhort and convict those who contradict.

The role of an elder is like that of a bishop. Both must meet the qualifications and their lives must reflect the standards and moral discipline of serving in these spiritual roles. A calling to shepherd the people of God is an honor indeed. It is job that requires humility and obedience to the word of God.

There is a reward for stepping into this role. As Paul writes, "Let the elders that rule well be counted worthy of double honor, especially they who labor in the word and doctrine. For the scripture saith, thou shalt not muzzle the ox that treadeth out the corn. And, the laborer is worthy of his reward" (1 Timothy 5:17–18).

Leading in a Crisis

In the early church, a crisis arose concerning the distribution of items to widows in the community. As we read in Acts, "Now in those days, when the number of the disciples was multiplying, there arose a complaint against the Hebrews by the Hellenists, because their widows were neglected in the daily distribution (Acts 6:1–2). The disciples, along with the deacons, needed to attend to an immediate issue that was causing a problem. In situations like this, the right individuals need to take command and accomplish the mission on the spot. The disciples determined they had the responsibility of attending to the word of God and ministering to the souls of men and women in their community. The need to serve tables was not part of that task; that needed to be delegated to the deacons. Let's examine this more closely.

Additionally in Acts, we read, "Therefore, brethren, seek out from among you seven men of good reputation, full of the Holy Spirit and wisdom, whom we may appoint over this business; but we will give ourselves continually to prayer and to the ministry of the word" (Acts 6:3–4). Not everyone is qualified or skilled to do all the things needed in ministry. It takes accountability, responsibility, and wisdom to ensure the right people are in the right roles and positions. Once the decision is made to move forward by putting a warm body in place, the work of the Lord moves forward. The selection of persons for the tasking was made after prayer was rendered unto God. It is imperative to seek God in placing those who are equipped and prepared for the work at hand. Prayer is necessary for all major matters and important appointments.

Crisis Management. One of the most revealing crises in Scripture is the Jethro and Moses crisis. In the reading there are areas of conflict, management, and leadership that are tackled and, in the materials methods, and systems are shared to clear the way for the issue at hand. The term conflict management is defined as "the practice of being able to identify conflicts sensibly, fairly, and efficiently." The scenario is that "Moses's father-in-law Jethro, along with Moses's wife and sons, came to him in the wilderness where he was camped at the mountain of God" (Exodus 18:5). Moses was exercising his responsibilities as the leader of the children of Israel. Once they all met, they had the normal, life-related conversations. Through the journey and conversation, Moses highlighted the triumphs and problems and also acknowledged the good God had done in their lives. Here is when the tide changed for Jethro.

> The next day Moses sat down to judge the people, and they stood around Moses from morning until evening. When Moses's father-in-law saw everything, he was doing for them he asked, "What is this you're doing for the people?" Why are you alone sitting as a judge, while all the people stand around you from morning until evening? (Exodus 18:13–14)

In moments like this, leadership and those in authority are challenged to help alleviate a problem that can spiral out of control. In Moses's heart, he felt what he was doing was the right thing. However, having someone on the outside objectively observing made it clear the practice was not good. How many of you can accept constructive criticism of a poor business or management behavior or practice? Here is where good crisis-conflict management arises. It is the application of strategies designed to help an organization deal with a sudden significant negative event. Jethro laid out a plan that would change Moses's conduct. In ministry, advice must be welcomed and accepted. Moses was serving the people in a good place but in the wrong way. As we read in Exodus, "'What you are doing is not good,' Moses's father-in-law said to him. 'You will certainly wear out both yourselves and these people who are with you because the task is too heavy for you. You can't do it alone'" (Exodus 18:17–18).

The Solution. The conflict was addressed and confronted. To handle it was a simple plan for a better resolution. In this crisis, Moses needed clear advice to assist him in making a better management decision. Managing people is not always an easy task. It takes honest and open communication to ensure everyone is heard and everyone concerned is listening. Exodus 18:21–22 reads,

> But you should select from all the people able men, God-fearing, trustworthy, and hating dishonest profit. Place them over the people as commanders of thousands, hundreds, fifties, and tens. They should always judge the people. Then they can bring you every major cause but judge every minor case themselves. In this way you will lighten your load, and they will bear it with you.

Ministry is not a job for the faint at heart. Jethro had the experience of speaking the right words into Moses's spirit. It takes a good listener to be a great follower. Exodus 18:23 reads, "If you do this, and God so directs you, you will be able to endure, and also all these people will be able to go home satisfied." In every organization, a caring and responsible leader wants everyone to return home satisfied. Our churches should be places where the word of God is coming forth with the power and strength of God. The souls who entered the doors may have entered one way but will leave in a better way and light. We know that "Moses listened to his father-in-law and did everything he said" (Exodus 18:24). A great solution was accomplished in the end.

Elders Called to Serve

In Acts 13:1–2, we read,

> In the church at Antioch there were certain prophets and teachers: Barnabas, Simeon who was called Niger, Lucius of Cyrene, Manaen who had been brought up with Herod the tetrarch, and Saul. As they ministered to the Lord and fasted, the Holy Spirit said, "Now separate to Me Barnabas and Saul for the work to which I have called them.

There are taskings in ministry that require prayer and fasting before moving forward in an assignment for God. The spiritual disciplines of prayer and fasting anoint the lives of the individuals tasked, and the impact is noted in the birthplace of their assignment. As we read in Acts, "Then, having fasted and prayed, and laid hands on them, they sent them away" (Acts 13:3). The blessings of God are bestowed upon a man or woman who has been called to serve in ministry. Jesus himself was on a mission when he sought out the twelve disciples for ministry. He selected ordinary, simple men whose hearts he could touch and who could move with compassion, empathy, and sensitivity among the people they would encounter. Can you be used by God to serve? Are you called to be an effective witness and servant in the work of the Lord?

Power, Authority, and Influence

Introduction

Power is defined as the ability to do something or act in a particular way. Authority is the power or right to give orders, make decisions, and enforce obedience. Lastly, influence is the capacity to influence the character, development, or behavior of someone or something, or the effect itself. There are many in the world today who seek power, not necessarily for the right reasons. Some seek to control, reign, or have positions or titles that bring them prestige, honor, and, more importantly, power of some kind. Of course, having power in one's life is not a negative trait or behavior. How well you handle the power that comes your way is important. Along with power comes authority. When you have authority, you have the final say in a major decision that can affect the future of a ministry, the present success of a ministry, and all the other elements that come along with having authority. Having authority, you become the one who ensures the payroll is in good shape, the bills are paid, the mortgage current, and other life areas are all in order. This brings us to the influence a leader has in the lives of those he or she reaches or connects with.

Jeremiah is a great example of someone whose life had meaning from birth. We read, "The word of the Lord came to me: I chose you before I formed you in the womb; I set you apart before you were born. I appointed you a prophet to the nations (Jeremiah 1:4–5). When God chooses you, it is a purpose beyond your reach. It is to be shared and exposed to the world. There are world leaders who appear in today's history books. You can become the next best for the influence, talent, and leadership inside of you. Jeremiah later expressed these words: "But I protested, 'Oh no, Lord God! Look, I don't know how to speak since I am only a youth.' Then the Lord said to me: Do not say, 'I am only a youth,' for you will go to everyone I send you to and speak whatever I tell you. Do not be afraid of anyone, for I will be with you to rescue you" (Jeremiah 1:6–8). It is revealing that the assignment upon Jeremiah's life began while he was in his youth. He didn't have the accolades or initials behind his name based on his academic successes. What he had was something all of us want in ministry: the influence and Spirit of God resting in our lives. The same authority and power given to him came with the understanding of being chosen for greatness, destiny, and having the influence of others.

A Mighty Man of Valor

It is one thing to have humility, not to think highly of ourselves, stay under the radar, and do the work you do as unto the Lord. There is a character in the Bible who fits this description quite well: Gideon. The angel of the Lord came, and he sat under the oak that was in Ophrah, which belonged to Joash, the Abiezrite. His son Gideon was threshing wheat in the winepress to hide it from the Midianites. Then the angel of the Lord appeared to him and said: "The Lord is with you, valiant warrior." When the hand of God is on you it's a blessing unlike none other. He further begins to express his unworthiness and inability to lead. Take note, "So he said to me, "This is the word of the Lord to Zerubbabel: 'Not by might nor by power, but by my Spirit, says the Lord Almighty (Zechariah 4:6 NIV). Gideon said to him, "Please, my Lord, if the Lord is with us, why has all this happened that our fathers told us about?" Fear and concern had been troubling Gideon, however, he didn't realize the grace and strength of God was over his life. God had a calling on Gideon's life. He knew he would be a person of great influence who would have an impact on others. God raises up people like Gideon to be voices for him.

John the Baptist, a voice crying in the wilderness, was a forerunner to spread a message of hope, deliverance, and salvation. Isaiah the prophet proclaimed these words about John: "See, I am sending my messenger ahead of you; he will prepare your way. A voice of one crying out in the wilderness. Prepare the way of the Lord, make his paths straight" (Mark 1:2–3). John the Baptist's life had a great impact before the entrance of Jesus Christ. As the forerunner, he was leading, affecting, empowering, and drawing souls to the kingdom of God. A notable characteristic about this powerful man was his humility. When people see you as a leader, one with power, charisma, and influence, your stake in the game rises to another level of respect. John's words explain this well: "One who is more powerful than I am is coming after me. I am not worthy to stoop down and untie the strap of his sandals. I baptize you with water, but he will baptize you with the Holy Spirit" (Mark 1:7). When a person can prefer another person over himself or herself, that is real humility. As we read in Romans, "Be devoted to one another in love. Honor one another above yourselves" (Romans 12:10).

Jesus Christ, the Son of the Living God

The culmination of power, authority, and influence covers an engaging and winning combination of the personality of a person who serves in ministry. The leadership needs to exercise the role of authority with passion and power at the same time. Leadership rises and falls from the top; therefore, someone has to take the responsibility for whatever happens. Only one person can exercise power, authority, and influence. As Matthew writes, "And Jesus came and spoke unto them, saying, 'All power is given unto Me in Heaven and on earth'" (Matthew 28:18). He is the main highlight of it all, the Alpha and Omega, the beginning, and the end. Jesus came to this earth to save people from their sins. He has the authority and power to save, heal, and forgive. His manner of reaching the lost and adding men and women to the church is demonstrated by the power and authority of the Word of God. Some will dispute the power and authority of the scriptures if they do not contain the words of Jesus, however, all scripture has his authority written in it. As 2 Timothy 3:16 states, "All Scripture is God-breathed and is useful for teaching, rebuking, correcting and training in righteousness."

Jesus's power was exemplified when he went to the cross of Calvary and rose again on the third day. He laid down his life for the entire world for the sins of many. As John writes, "Greater love has no one than this: to lay down one's life for one's friends" (John 15: 13). He loved the world that much. Yet, He knew he was going to rise from the grave. The first letter of Paul to the Corinthians reads, "For I delivered unto you first of all that which I also received, how Christ died for our sins according to the Scriptures; and that He was buried, and that he rose again the third day according to the scriptures" (1 Corinthians 15:3–4). In his triumphal reign, one day it will all be over, it will all come to an end. All who have a hope in Christ look for his return with great expectation. Paul adds, "Then cometh the end, when he shall have delivered up the kingdom of God, even the Father, when he shall have put down all rule and all authority and power" (1 Corinthians 15:24).

In closing, one verse can bring clarity of the power and authority of Jesus Christ in these simple words: "For unto us a child is born, unto us a son is given: and the government shall be upon his shoulder: and his name shall be called Wonderful, Counsellor, The mighty God, The everlasting Father, The Prince of Peace" (Isaiah 9:6).

Walking in Humility

In a world of popularity, Facebook, Instagram, TikTok, Twitter, and other social media platforms, an individual can become an overnight sensation by garnering a lot of recognition or likes. In that case, an unknown name becomes popular and spoken of by the world. How does this happen? In this twenty-first century, social media is fast-growing. However, in the days of Jesus Christ, there were no social media platforms, yet he was one of the most popular and well-known figures in all the earth. No viral videos went into cyberspace and made him famous. It wasn't getting likes and shared posts that spread his name abroad; it was the works and many miracles he performed that made all this possible. As Mark recounts, "They were all amazed, and so they began to ask each other 'What is this? A new teaching with authority! He commands even unclean spirits, and they obey him. At once the news about him spread throughout the entire vicinity of Galilee'" (Mark 1:27–28). This is what power, authority and influence looked like in a man who exemplified true humility. As you grow and come through the ranks of ministry and leadership, model your path to success on the life and example Jesus Christ has set for the world to know. As Paul writes,

> Rather, he made himself nothing by taking the very nature of a servant, being made in human likeness. And being found in appearance as a man, he humbled himself by becoming obedient to death even death on a cross! Therefore, God exalted him to the highest place and gave him

the name that is above every name. (Philippians 2:7–9).

How you live and how you engage with others will be the doors that open many opportunities to make a difference in the lives of the people you meet.

In closing, the words of Jesus Christ provide a great summation of influence: "And I, when I am lifted up from the earth, will draw all people to myself" (John 12:32).

Major Management Arteries of the Church and Congregational Life

Introduction

One Bible verse speaks about the church's arteries and how they impact the congregation and the management of the house of God. We read in 1 Timothy, "These things I write to you shortly; but if I am delayed, I write so that you may know how you ought to conduct yourself in the house of God, which is the pillar and ground of the truth. And without controversy great is the mystery of godliness" (1 Timothy 3:14–16). It takes a concerted effort of pulling together the best minds, the best processes, and best stewards who are gifted and mindful of the necessity of doing all things well for the work of ministry. The spirit of excellence is doing things well, decently, and in order. Serving in excellence is not about being competitive or seeking the applause of people; it is about doing the best work for God. One should never just do a work for God carelessly or with a lack of great effort. The great word of Solomon expresses our energy toward the work of God like this: "Whatsoever your hands finds to do, do it with all your might; for there is no activity or planning or knowledge or wisdom in Sheol (the nether world, the place of the dead) where you are going" (Ecclesiastes 9:10).

A great model of excellent behavior is from the prophet

Daniel. We read, "Then Daniel distinguished himself above the governors and satraps, because an excellent spirit was in him, and the king gave thought to setting him over the whole realm" (Daniel 6:3–4). Service excellence refers to the ability of service providers to consistently meet, and sometimes even exceed, customer expectations. Daniel demonstrated wisdom, knowledge, and the ability to oversee a whole infrastructure. Daniel was able to do what he knew best to avoid compromising his spiritual stand and faith in God. He abstained from eating food from the king's table by eating fruits and vegetables for ten days. This decision proved to be good for his entire team as well. Team leadership is important. Daniel provided guidance, instruction, direction, and leadership to a group of individuals. With this mindset, I will explore the right pieces of a successful organization.

A Connected Congregation

A congregation must have the same energy and passion to bring the congregation into alignment with the word of God. There cannot be a power struggle for everyone seeking to lead or be in charge. There should be a good, natural blend and acknowledgment of the strengths and weaknesses of all concerned. Strengths bring the best of resources, tools, and ideas to the table. The weaknesses show the need to have others to join in moving things and the congregation in the right direction. What is the key ingredient of bringing the congregation together? Faith. Faith is defined as "complete trust or confidence in someone or something." The word of God states, "Until we all reach unity in the faith and in the knowledge of the Son of God and become mature, attaining to the whole measure of the fullness of Christ" (Ephesians 4:13). One word that can be challenged in this verse is *mature*. Maturity is necessary to bring quality and success to the body of a congregation. As we read in the Book of James,

"Let perseverance finish its work so that you may be mature and complete, not lacking anything" (James 1:4). Having mature leaders and workers serving in ministry assures nothing will be lacking. It is important for accountability and control to be fully engaged in the house of God. Maturing and accountability go hand in hand. You can't have one without the other.

How does one ensure a congregation is connected? A congregation must be unified. It must have the self-awareness to keep the needle moving in the right direction. There has to be a mechanism and drive to keep the main thing the main thing to achieve a goal. For so long, many people have quoted these words as if they are written in the Bible: "Where there is unity, there is strength." This sounds good, but it is not biblical. However, there is a verse in the Bible about unity; Psalm 133 states, "Behold, how good and how pleasant it is for brethren to dwell together in unity" (Psalm 133:1).

Setting the Example

A congregation must have mature men and women in place to model the behavior it wants to see among the congregation. Paul addresses the importance of women and aged men taking on the roles and behaviors that represent the life of a Christian well.

> Likewise, teach the older women to be reverent in the way they live, not to be slanderers, or addicted to much wine, but to teach what is good. Then they can urge the younger women to love their husbands and children, to be self-controlled and pure, to be busy at home, to be kind, and to be subject to their husbands, so that no one will malign the word of God. (Titus 2:3–5)

There are different age groups in a congregation. The older individuals are pillars and mainstays who have good foundational principles.

Titus 2:2 states, "Teach the older men to be temperate, worthy of respect, self-controlled, and sound in faith in love and in endurance." Paul also addresses the conduct of young men in the congregation life, writing, "Similarly, encourage the young men to be self-controlled. In everything set them an example by doing what is good. In your teaching show integrity, seriousness and soundness of speech that cannot be condemned, so that those who oppose you may be ashamed because they have nothing bad to say about us" (Titus 2:6–8).

Let's address the seventh verse out of this reading a little closer. If setting the example is important and significant for being a light in a dark world, holding up standards and good moral values that comes along with good character, it speaks clearly to how this is handled. Titus 2:7 reads, "In all things showing thyself a pattern of good works: in doctrine showing uncorruptness, gravity sincerity." A pattern is "a model or design used as a guide in needlework and other crafts." The world looks for role models in the sports arena, the music arena, and other places that draw an audience. Ministry needs role models. I'm not talking about being like Mike; I'm talking about standing tall as an ambassador for Christ. Mark writes, "Mark the perfect man and behold the upright: for the end of that man is peace" (Mark 37:37). This includes peace in how you engage with others, how you conduct business affairs, and peace in your life. This behavior covers a large part of your life. You will engage in sound biblical doctrine that cannot be condemned. Your standard indicates things you will not yield to or fall to. Your level of sincerity and gravity will represent you well.

In a previous reading in this book, Jesus compares a person in a congregation to "salt" and "light." If there was ever a time for people to stand tall and come to the forefront in an ever-changing world to represent the light of Jesus Christ, it is now. Matthew recounts, "You are the salt of the earth but if the salt loses its saltiness, how can it be made salty again? It is no longer good for anything, except to be thrown out and trampled underfoot" (Matthews 5:13). The salt adds the substance and the evidence of being good for the body of Christ. When it becomes unsalted, it is no longer effective and accomplishing its intended purpose. The last thing the church wants to do is lose anyone. All souls are important for the growth and unity of the church.

Lastly, *you* are the light of the world (Matthew 5:14). As we read in the Gospel of Matthew, "Let your light shine before others, that they may see your good deeds and glorify your Father in heaven" (Matthew 5:16)

A Chosen Vessel

To maintain the proper functioning of the church's arteries in handling the daily affairs of ministry, the right man or woman must be at the helm of things. In the secular world, an organization's human resources department defines the strategic approach to the effective and efficient management of people in the organization. The strategy maximizes employee performance in service of an employer's strategic objective. Looking at this perspective, one may ask, "How does this apply to church management or maximize the work of ministry?" This is a great question. I'm glad you asked.

The Gentiles needed to hear the gospel of Jesus Christ. God knew that for this to be accomplished, he needed the right man to reach the masses. He needed someone to cry out and reach for the souls of men and women to change. Paul did not love God. He wanted to cast those who called on God into prison. Acts 9:1–2 tells us, "Now Saul was still breathing threats and murder against the disciples of the Lord. He went to the high priest and requested letters from him to the synagogues in Damascus, so that if he found any men or women who belonged to the Way, he might bring them as prisoners to Jerusalem."

A heart change took place in the process of wanting to do harm. While he was traveling on the Damascus road, a light shined from Heaven and changed the course of Saul's life. His name was changed to Paul forever. When God has need of you, he knows how to get your attention. The story of Paul depicts many life lessons in becoming the vessel God chooses to work for him. Ministries choose vessels to see growth, to see the potential of others taking charge, to make sound decisions, and to exercise good business practices. Should the term business be affiliated with the church? Romans 12:11 reads, "Not slothful in business; fervent in spirit; serving the Lord." It is about serving and giving your best to the work of ministry.

Joshua faced a life-changing moment after the death of Moses, the one who led the children of Israel in the wilderness. Let's look at the words God shared with this leader.

> Be strong and courageous, for you will distribute the land I swore to their ancestors to give them as an inheritance. Above all, be strong and very courageous to observe carefully the whole instruction my servant Moses commanded you. Do not turn from it to the right or left, so that you will have success wherever you go. (Joshua 1:6–7).

Joshua needed to let the word of God be his resource of strategy, preparedness, and wealth of success. It was the book of instruction. Every CEO needs policies and good management procedures in place. This passage closes out with the words, "For then you will prosper and succeed in whatever you do" (Joshua 1:8).

Pastors must have hearts of ministry to lead the charge to

serve the people of God. Loving your family, your spouse, and your children must all be aligned with the work and tasks assigned to your hands. A disciplined prayer life, reading the word of God, and other spiritual disciplines should be routine and practiced with fervent intensity and heart. A passage from Jeremiah sums this book's content in these few words: "And I will give them one heart, and one way, that they may fear me for ever, for the good of them, and of their children after them" (Jeremiah 32:39).

Biography

Dr. Terence O. Hayes, Sr. serves as the Senior Pastor of Faith Deliverance Church of God in Christ with eighteen years of leadership. He is a leader with a heart for the people and desire to have an impact in their everyday lives through preaching and teaching the gospel message of Jesus Christ. Terence served over twenty-one years in the United States Air Force and retired in July 2002. He served twenty years at Wright Patterson Air Force Base as an administrative specialist. He completed a one-year tour in the Republic of Korea at Osan Air Base as an executive officer. Upon his retirement, he was awarded several distinctive medals, including the Meritorious Service Medal, the Outstanding Volunteer Service Medal, and the Air Force Commendation Medal with five oak leaf clusters.

His astute administrative skills, contagious personality, and willingness to serve God and his congregation are testaments to his heartfelt leadership skills. Pastor Hayes's favorite passage of scripture is, "Where there is no vision, the people would perish: but he that keepeth the law, happy is he" (Proverbs 29:18).

Terence is a bi-vocational pastor, currently a supply technician for foreign military sales at Wright Patterson Air Force Base, Ohio, and an Adjunct Professor at Liberty University. He is a graduate of Liberty University with an educational doctoral degree in community care and counseling, with a cognate in pastoral counseling. He also holds a Master of Arts in pastoral counseling, a Bachelor of Science degree in psychology with a concentration in Christian counseling, and an associate's degree in psychology and Christian counseling. In 2014, he was selected as one of the Church of God in Christ's 100 Influential Pastors. In 2021, Liberty University awarded Terence the Founding Dean Integration Award. Terence received the Dr. Martin Luther King Humanitarian Award in February of 2021 from Wright Patterson Air Force Base, Ohio. In 2021, he released his first published book, *Resilience, and Success of African American Pastors: A Phenomenological Investigation*. Mental health is a passion in his life. In memory of his late mother, he established and funded the Ethel Hayes Destigmatization of Mental Health Scholarship with a non-profit organization, www.bold.org He's also a member of the American Association of Christian Counselors and the Society for Collegiate Leadership and Achievement.

Terence is married to Rhonda L. McDuffie-Hayes. They were joined in holy matrimony on January 26, 1980. They are the proud parents of five daughters and two sons, three sons-in-law, two daughters-in-law, and a host of grandchildren.

The Heart of Ministry (A Candid Interview with Dr. Hayes)

1. What made you have the assurance that God called you for ministry?

I accepted my calling in the ministry after completing my basic training in the United States Air Force. In my youth, I loved serving in the church as a junior deacon and a devotional leader, now known as a praise and worship leader. I also served as a teacher at a very young age, teaching the adults at the local church I attended. Looking at the five-fold ministry, I saw myself as a pastor/teacher. My prayer was for God to bless me to come through in basic training, and I wanted to give my life towards the work of ministry.

2. How has education impacted or affected your calling as a pastor?

The educational journey for me embraces all the questions above. My exposure to some theology classes gave me an inside view of studying the word of God with a textbook point of view of scripturally based text. The more I studied, the more it increased my desire to learn more and to grow spiritually. I sought a more precise worldview of ministry and how the word of God impacts the lives of people who are introduced to the gospel of Jesus Christ. I further saw the educational experience as something to add to my spiritual life to further the cause of the gospel.

3. What sparked the passion in you to enter ministry and seek the role of senior pastor?

Loving people. To serve as a pastor, you must love people, and the flaws, the weaknesses, the strengths, and all the things that come along with human nature. People need a shepherd who will lead them and instruct them from the oracles of the word of God. Many people take an interest in ministry, but their hearts can be elsewhere. I wanted to give my all to the work of the ministry. Ministry is about seeing men and women coming to Christ, which will increase the kingdom. Lastly, pastors must be servants. Serving people is what Christ Jesus did, and I, again, love people.

4. How do you define success in ministry and being a professional?

Success is seeing the growth and maturity of the men and women you teach and instruct in a ministry. The word of God is the method of instruction in how to live and become a true disciple of Christ. I don't measure the success of the ministry by the membership numbers. Effectiveness measures something numbers cannot.

5. Why is being ordained vital to you in ministry?

Ordination is the seal of being called to become a minister/elder, which can turn into the subsequent role of pastor. The certification of the organization that is six-million strong adds a sense of satisfaction and completion of the work of ministry. This is the fulfillment of being called into ministry.

6. What are the signs of ministry that provoked you to be successful?

I inherited my work as a pastor from the former pastor. The ministry had been functioning well for twenty-four years. I wanted to continue the work positively and keep it from going down or becoming obsolete. Once I was appointed as a pastor, I took the job on day one prepared to give the best of me to make it the best to give to God.

7. What infrastructures did you put in place to help you stay the task in ministry, both naturally and spiritually?

I put in place all the taskings listed here: prayer, solid biblical studies in the tradition of Sunday School, and other biblical learning areas. Music is a strong presence in our ministry. I was devoted to a musical group I developed known as New Harvest, which became a three-time Dove Award nominee. I took my passion as a musical artist and carried it into the role of ministry. I even included it in our motto: "the place where ministry, music, and the saving of souls is our goal." The word *infrastructures* takes me to my days of military training. I wanted a well-organized and structured ministry that flowed well and was meaningful and purposeful for the congregation. I wanted to train, equip, and empower.

8. How does establishing an inner circle of other pastors in your circle of ministry help you?

An inner circle is critical to me. In ministry, pastors need one another. This can be a lonely place. Having an inner circle provides you a chance to share in a safe place the burdens of ministry. It also allows you to have someone to share your heart with if there are any struggles or challenges you may be encountering. Jesus's model of Peter, James, and John is a great example; if he had men whom he leaned on and called upon, pastors, too, need that same engagement.

9. What preparations have you made to serve as a senior pastor?

The first preparation I made as a pastor was to seek the face of God. I wanted to know my place and responsibility in leading the flock of God. I never wanted to take ownership, to say, "my ministry." I am the undershepherd of God's flock. I recall the year I decided to pursue the educational goals and I was appointed pastor. I was enrolled, had my classes aligned, and was ready to go. However, I stopped before I began. I said, "I don't know what it's going to be like becoming a pastor; this can wait." Fast forward, and it was the best delay I could have ever imagined. First, I was going to pursue a business administration degree because of my background in administration in the military. When I did return to education, I sought God, prayed about it, and was led to enter Christian counseling and psychology. It was the best decision I could have ever made. I wanted to be aware of the behavior of the people I served. It gave me great sensitivity and empathy for the lives of men and women from all walks of life.

10. How did you navigate through challenging moments in your ministry?

This question is powerful to me. I navigated through challenging moments by standing on the word of God, but I embraced one character in the Bible: Nehemiah. His leadership, tenacity, resilience, and focused attitude impacted my thinking. It appeared he encountered problems in his role, just as pastors do in ours. This book became a go-to reference for me and made a significant impact on my life. There were days I felt like quitting, not on God, just in the role of the pastor. When you inherit a ministry, there are many factors you may encounter, including loyalty, acceptance, and walking into your own identity. Through prayer and trusting God, I survived it all.

11. How important is family life for you as a pastor?

Family life is essential. If you cannot manage your own house, how can you handle the house of God? I love that I have a beautiful wife and seven children, and I became a pastor when the children were older. The time given to a body in ministry can consume your family time; therefore, keeping the balance and the family in front makes a difference. My children engaged in roles in good ministry. They assisted me in areas that needed to be occupied. In many instances, wives may pursue roles in a ministry with their husbands, but my wife's presence speaks loudly just being in the midst. She is an excellent model of a kind, caring, and loving wife and mother. She provides welcomes in the women's services and assists in setting up events—a helper role in ministry.

12. How necessary are finances to establish a ministry?

Finances are most definitely important. You can't do ministry successfully without finances. Furthermore, good stewardship is a must. The ministry must survive, and the needs of the ministry must be met. You can't be frugal. God's house should have the best of everything. Follow the principles of giving from the word of God and he will bless your work every time. I burned the mortgage of our $510,000 complex during the pandemic of 2020. The people of the ministry sowed in the good ground and made it happen. When people see what you're doing with finances, they are more willing to give.

Bibliography

Printed in the United States
by Baker & Taylor Publisher Services